LIGHTNING FROM THE COCKPIT

LIGHTNING
FROM
THE COCKPIT

Peter Caygill

Pen & Sword
AVIATION

First published in Great Britain in 2004
and reprinted in paperback format in 2006, 2011, and 2013 by
PEN & SWORD AVIATION
An imprint of
Pen & Sword Books Ltd
47 Church Street
Barnsley
South Yorkshire
S70 2AS

ISBN 978 1 84415 355 8

Printed and bound in England
By CPI Group (UK) Ltd, Croydon, CR0 4YY

Pen & Sword Books Ltd incorporates the Imprints of Pen & Sword Aviation,
Pen & Sword Family History, Pen & Sword Maritime, Pen & Sword Military,
Pen & Sword Discovery, Pen & Sword Politics, Pen & Sword Atlas,
Pen & Sword Archaeology, Wharncliffe Local History, Wharncliffe True Crime,
Wharncliffe Transport, Pen & Sword Select, Pen & Sword Military Classics,
Leo Cooper, The Praetorian Press, Claymore Press, Remember When,
Seaforth Publishing and Frontline Publishing

For a complete list of Pen & Sword titles please contact
PEN & SWORD BOOKS LIMITED
47 Church Street, Barnsley, South Yorkshire, S70 2AS, England
E-mail: enquiries@pen-and-sword.co.uk
Website: www.pen-and-sword.co.uk

Contents

Acknowledgements

I t would not have been possible to write a book of this nature without the help and enthusiastic support of a number of former Lightning pilots, and I should like to thank them for sharing their experiences with me. In alphabetical order they are as follows:

Wing Commander Martin Bee AFC
Wing Commander Brian Carroll
Group Captain Graham Clarke
Air Commodore Ken Goodwin CBE AFC
Air Vice-Marshal 'Paddy' Harbison CB CBE AFC
Squadron Leader Wally Hill
Squadron Leader David Jones
Flight Lieutenant Trevor MacDonald-Bennett
Squadron Leader Henryk Ploszek AFC
Group Captain John Robertson
Group Captain Dave Roome OBE
Group Captain Mike Shaw CBE
Air Commodore David Simmons CBE AFC MA
Flight Lieutenant Geoff Steggall
Group Captain Peter Vangucci AFC

Once again I am deeply indebted to Bob Cossey of the 74 (F) Tiger Squadron Association for putting me in touch with many of the pilots named above, and to Brian Carroll for providing much material relating to his long career on Lightnings that amounted to 3,000 hours flying time. My special thanks also go to Wing Commander Anthony 'Bugs' Bendell OBE, AFC for allowing me to quote from his autobiography 'Never In Anger', and to Philip Jarrett who supplied many of the photographs. Much research was carried out at the National Archives at Kew, and I should like to thank the staff for their assistance and applaud a superbly efficient organization that delivers documents to readers so quickly.

Finally my thanks must go to my wife Mel, and daughter Anna, for putting up with my long absences in the study and early morning departures to London.

Introduction

On a cold, grey day in March 1964 I was walking along a country lane close to RAF Leeming in North Yorkshire when a Lightning F.1 of 226 OCU flew overhead, having carried out a practice approach to Runway 34. It climbed to around 2,000 ft before turning towards the north-east, soon becoming just a speck in the sky. I watched until it was out of sight and then turned and trudged dejectedly back home. The Lightnings were regular visitors at Leeming, but only a few days before it had been announced that their base at nearby Middleton St George was to close and the OCU was to move to Coltishall, near Norwich. For an eleven-year-old aircraft spotter, they might as well have been moving to the other side of the world. Suddenly the prospect of being able to watch nothing more exciting than a succession of Jet Provosts, grinding out endless circuits, seemed appalling. I might have felt a little better had I known that the Lightning would remain in service for another twenty-four years, but the fact that 'my' aircraft were leaving was hard to take.

Just as it was the enthusiast's favourite, the Lightning was also top of the list for those pilots lucky enough to fly it. It was a quintessentially British fighter, short on fuel, but with plenty of power and an absolute delight to fly. At the time of its inception, its performance put it into a different league altogether, and it was to remain ahead of the rest in this respect until the arrival of the F-15 and F-16 in the 1970s. The Lightning was anything but 'digital', and it represented the zenith of old-style technology, the main 'computer' being situated between the pilot's ears. This invariably meant an extremely high cockpit workload, but the satisfaction from achieving a successful kill in marginal weather, with rapidly dwindling fuel reserves, was immense. Against all the odds the Lightning was not retired from first-line duties until 1988, a fact that speaks volumes for the skill of the team at English Electric and the dedication and professionalism of the RAF.

Much has been written about the Lightning but very few books have concentrated on the handling and performance aspects of the aircraft. Early publications tended to be rather vague when it came to quoting performance figures with liberal use of words such as 'estimated' and 'approximately' or just a blunt 'no details available for publication'. The popular press only served to confuse the issue by reporting that Lightnings had stunned USAF U-2 pilots by sitting 'effortlessly' on their tails during practice interceptions at heights of 60,000 ft and above. Only in recent years has it been possible to ascertain the true performance levels and methods of operation of the Lightning with the gradual release of classified documents. These, and the testimony of pilots who flew the Lightning, give a fascinating insight into one of the most charismatic combat aircraft of all time.

Although the Lightning was retired from service sixteen years ago, the legend lives on. At the time of writing the RAF is set to receive the Eurofighter Typhoon, a modern day equivalent, but it seems unlikely that it will acquire the same aura. Described by one pilot as 'a dinky little aeroplane with highly efficient but gutless engines' it has a lot to live up to, and for many the Lightning will remain simply the best. Barring any dramatic U-turns by the Civil Aviation Authority however, British enthusiasts now really do have to go to the other side of the world to see one fly!

CHAPTER ONE

The P.1A at Boscombe Down

The airfield at Boscombe Down, just to the south-east of Amesbury in Wiltshire, has been the setting for some momentous events in the history of British military aviation, but the first flight of the English Electric P.1A WG760 on 4 August 1954 was especially significant. It was flown on this occasion by Roland Beamont (English Electric's Chief Test Pilot) and in a few short minutes it became clear that the design philosophy used by W.E.W. Petter, the company's Chief Engineer, had been based on sound principles and that developments would be capable of restoring the UK's reputation as a builder of state-of-the-art interceptors, a situation that had been taken for granted until the political meddling of the first post-war Labour government. It also represented a second resounding success for the fledgling design team, who were also responsible for the Canberra twin-jet bomber.

Although an outstanding success, that first flight was not without its problems. R/T failure and deteriorating weather had caused some concern, together with insufficient nose-down trim and heavy buffet when the dive brakes were extended. However, Beamont's confidence in the aircraft was expressed only a week later when he took the P.1A above Mach 1 to become the first pilot to fly a British aircraft at supersonic speed in level flight. Despite the fact that the P.1A had a radical planform, in terms of construction and systems it was relatively conventional. This resulted in very few lay-ups and a high sortie rate. WG760 was returned to the English Electric test airfield at Warton on 23 September 1954, and the flight envelope expanded further so that Mach 1.24 had been achieved by the end of the year. The longitudinal trimming difficulties were quickly overcome, although the dive brakes were to remain a problem for some time to come.

By early 1955 it was considered that the P.1A had been developed sufficiently for it to be flown by Aeroplane and Armament Experimental

Establishment (A&AEE) pilots, and the aircraft returned to Boscombe Down in March. By this time total flying time was forty-nine hours in seventy-six sorties, a further thirteen flights being made during the preview assessment. All-up weight of WG760 was 27,100 lb, and it was fitted with Sapphire Sa.5 engines uprated almost to Sa.6 standard, with reheat rings fitted but inoperative. Operations were restricted as the flutter/flight resonance test programme had not been completed. Airframe limitations were as follows:

0–12,500 ft	480 kts IAS
12,500–25,000 ft	0.9 IMN
25,000–30,000 ft	450 kts IAS
30,000 ft +	1.15 IMN
Flaps down	235 kts IAS
Undercarriage down	250 kts IAS
Minimum airspeed	150 kts IAS
Maximum height	48,000 ft (pending mods to pressure cabin altitude limit)
Max normal acceleration	+4 g
Airbrakes	Only to be used in emergency due to severe nose-up trim change and heavy buffet
Rolls	180 deg/sec (360 degrees total travel in any one roll)

Engine limitations were:

	Duration (min)	rpm	Tolerance (rpm)	JPT°C
Take-off and combat	10	8,600	±50	665
Intermediate	30	8,400	–	625
Max continuous	Unlimited	8,200	–	585
Min approach	Unlimited	5,000	–	560
Ground idling	Unlimited	3,000	+200, -0	560

These limitations, together with inadequate thrust above 40,000 ft and the 'rather sparse' fuel allowances, severely affected the scope of the test, which was confined to assessing general handling characteristics. Even so, a time of four minutes from wheels rolling to 40,000 ft and 1.0 TMN in level flight at this altitude was way in advance of any aircraft previously tested.

Handling of the P.1A on the ground was relatively straightforward. Good brakes and a wide-track undercarriage made for easy turning, although this was marred slightly by a large break-out force on the nose-wheel castoring unit. High engine rpm was required to get the aircraft moving, but once rolling, the minimum requirement of 4,000 rpm for each engine to keep the generators charging caused some embarrassment as a fast taxiing speed soon built up.

Take-off was made using -5 degrees of tailplane trim and no flap. Full thrust (8,600 rpm) could be held on the brakes on dry concrete, but they were normally released at 7,500 rpm. There was a slight tendency to weathercock in crosswinds, and a little corrective brake was occasionally needed to keep straight at low speeds. Acceleration was rapid, the rudder becoming effective early in the take-off run. Tailplane control came in at about 100 kts IAS, and when the nose was raised at about 120 kts IAS care had to be taken not to let it rise too sharply. At this point the acceleration was very rapid, the aircraft normally being eased off the ground at 170 kts IAS in a markedly nose-up attitude. The ailerons were very responsive, and it was possible to induce a lateral oscillation, which, if encountered, was best dealt with by making no attempt at correction as this only made matters worse. The rate of undercarriage retraction was rapid and a slight residual nose-up trim change was noted.

The P.1A's attitude in the climb was very steep and difficulty was experienced in keeping to the correct IAS and Mach number limits owing to inadequate pitch information from the artificial horizon. This situation was aggravated by badly synchronized throttles and a slight lag in tailplane response. Tailplane trim set to -5 degrees was found to be suitable for the whole subsonic speed range except when flaps and undercarriage were down. Between 0.95 and 1.00 TMN there was a steady nose-down trim change which required +2 degrees of tailplane trim to restore balance. When decelerating between 0.98 and 0.96 TMN under applied 'g', the reverse happened and there was a small but sudden nose-up pitch which was usually over before the pilot had time to react to it. The increment in 'g' was never more than 0.75 at high altitude, which was not considered serious and could in no way be compared to the 'pitch up' experienced by certain other 45-degree swept-wing fighters, in particular the Supermarine Swift.

Aileron over-sensitivity was also apparent at 0.94–0.96 IMN, and it was thought that formation flying would have been difficult. This was in spite of modifications carried out by English Electric that had resulted in a doubling of the stick force at full travel. Non-linear stick gearing was also introduced, the aim being to eradicate the almost continuous rolling oscillation that had been encountered during early test flights. Considering the need for adequate rolling power over a wide speed range, it was felt that the residual over-sensitivity at high subsonic speeds was not entirely unexpected.

Rolling was restricted to 180 deg/sec because of wing-tank fuel pressures and to 360 deg/sec total rotation because of the possibility of divergence in yaw arising from inertia coupling. This was not noticed during testing, and the aircraft also showed no tendency to self-induced Dutch rolling or snaking. However, during investigation of the damping characteristics of lateral and directional oscillations, it was found that the roll to yaw ratio was relatively high and the oscillation was not particularly well damped. A degree of heaviness was also noted in longitudinal control at transonic speeds.

During manoeuvring at transonic speeds a certain amount of aero-dynamic 'buzz' was encountered, and a steep spiral descent had to be performed to maintain constant Mach number when increasing 'g'. This pointed to high levels of induced drag in manoeuvring flight, but until the flight envelope had been extended it was not possible to investigate further.

On the approach to land the wheels were lowered at 230 kts IAS, at which point there were a series of lateral and longitudinal trim changes culminating in a change to nose-down. From this speed down to 160 kts IAS the aircraft was comfortable to fly, although rudder had to be used to co-ordinate turns. It was found that the rudder was also very sensi-tive and it was easy to over-control. With the nose flaps lowered there was a very slight nose-down change in attitude, but with the trailing edge flaps fully down this trim change became much more pronounced and a large increase in power was required to maintain the correct flight path. In this condition directional control was less touchy.

Care had to be taken not to lose speed during the final turn in for the approach, which was made at 190 kts IAS, requiring a relatively large proportion of total power. The approach angle was flat and speed was reduced so that the aircraft crossed the boundary at 165 kts IAS, when the throttles were closed and the stick eased gently back. Touchdown was made after a period of float. During this time there was no wing dropping in crosswinds, but the streaming of the tail parachute in such conditions induced a noticeable yaw into wind.

Despite the fact that the trial had been heavily restricted, the aircraft's potential was clearly apparent. Considering the trauma that the British aircraft industry had gone through when investigating the transonic

region of flight, it was heartening to read words such as 'straightforward', 'pleasant' and 'docile' in the A&AEE report on the P.1A. No
problems were envisaged as regards conversion to type – all the aircraft
needed was a lot more power and a lot more fuel. The former would be
available in abundance with the Rolls-Royce-Avon-powered P.1B.
However, the latter would remain as one of the type's weak points
throughout its time in service.

A second assessment was carried out at Boscombe Down in
November 1955, by which time WG760 had been modified in several
respects. In the intervening months English Electric had experimented
with leading-edge notches to inhibit the spanwise flow of air over the
60-degree swept wing. By cutting the width of the notch to 1.85 inches
(from 3.5 inches) it was found that the buffet threshold was extended
and there was also a reduction in the aileron over-sensitivity. The
leading-edge flaps were also made inoperative as flight-testing had
shown them to be of little value. Modifications were also made to the
tailplane feel system by incorporating some spring feel for emergency
purposes in the event of hydraulic failure, and the aileron feel was also
modified, the spring rate being increased to 18 lb instead of 12 lb stick
force for full stick displacement.

Flight limitations had been raised to a maximum of 600 kts IAS or
1.3 M (whichever was the lower), and the normal acceleration limit was
5 g at subsonic speeds below 500 kts IAS, with 3 g above this speed, and
at supersonic speeds. An additional restriction was imposed of 400 kts
IAS and 0.9 IMN when flying with the hydraulic feel simulators
inoperative. Engine limits were unchanged.

No new points were raised during the second assessment, which
generally agreed with the findings of the first preview. Pilots still found
difficulty with the steep attitude and rapid rate of climb after take-off,
which was too much for the instruments, and it was relatively easy to
exceed the recommended climbing speed of 450 kts IAS. During the
approach and landing the fixing of the leading-edge flaps made no
difference to the aircraft's handling characteristics.

The nosing-up tendency still occurred when decelerating through
0.95 M under 'g', and although not serious, it was felt that gun aiming
would be impossible in this region. However, A&AEE still thought it
'commendable that any peculiarities arising from compressibility have
been confined to this relatively narrow band of flight speeds'. The
reduction in the size of the leading-edge notches produced a noticeable
delay in the onset of 'buzz', which had been apparent at very low values
of lift coefficient (CL) during the first preview. On several occasions
pilots reported signs of stick force lightening during steep turns where
high values of 'g' were applied, a characteristic which may have been

caused by fuel shifting rearwards in the wing tanks as the turn was tightened.

Throughout the speed range up to 600 kts IAS at low level and up to 1.3 TMN at high altitude, the ailerons were found to be very effective, with good response, and there was no indication of the previous over-sensitivity. Such was the confidence in the aircraft's lateral control that hesitation rolls were carried out with precision at 1.15 IMN. Tailplane control, although effective, did not have good response. It was best at high IAS, but deteriorated with decreasing IAS and at supersonic speeds. As a result of this characteristic, pilots new to the P.1A were prone to over-control after take-off, which led to a certain amount of 'pump handling'. At 0.94–0.97 IMN, however, longitudinal control was sensitive and touchy. The rudder was effective with adequate response at all speeds, although it became so heavy at high IAS as to be virtually immovable.

During the trial WG760 was flown by two pilots from the Air Fighting Development Squadron (AFDS), part of the Central Fighter Establishment (CFE) at West Raynham. These were Wg Cdr J.L.W. Ellacombe DFC and Sqn Ldr A.D. Woodcock, who between them flew seven sorties. Their participation in the assessment was dogged by a fair amount of bad luck. A week was lost when a compressor in one of the engines disintegrated, and then Woodcock hit a plover on take-off, which required a double engine change. Delays were also experienced waiting for good weather, as it was felt that the inadequacies of the blind-flying instruments after take-off posed an unacceptable risk.

Ellacombe and Woodcock were highly impressed with the P.1A. The conclusions to their report were as follows:

> The aircraft is very pleasant to fly throughout the speed range and it is considered that this is a useable aircraft which Fighter Command pilots will like. There is no doubt that the higher speeds and the added complication of pilot-operated AI is going to call for a high standard of flying to obtain the maximum results from the F.23 [the P.1A was built to Specification F.23/49]. However, it is the opinion of the author that the good average pilot with a couple of years' operational experience and about 500–600 hours flying will be able to cope with the higher standards required. Efficient simulators will greatly assist in pilot training.
>
> There are several features of the P.1A that call for favourable comment. Having two engines there is the added safety factor in the event of an engine failure. Furthermore, the two engines provide independent generators and a duplicated hydraulic system with separate hydraulic pumps. The effectiveness of the

tail parachute further emphasizes the need to equip our present high-pressure-tyred aircraft with tail parachutes, both to cut down tyre wear and to operate off runways when they are marginal with ice or heavy rain. The cockpit heating, canopy and windscreen demisting systems are excellent. In addition, there is an emergency supply which supplies ram air into the cockpit, and this should cater for the most extreme misting conditions. The elevator and aileron control systems are the most effective experienced to date. This experience includes Hunter, Swift, F-84 and F-86E Sabre.

With regard to the P.1A's handling characteristics in the upper part of its speed range the A& AEE report had the following to say:

Transonic Handling – Up to 0.94 M the handling was normal, the ailerons were responsive and very effective, the tailplane was effective but had a lower than expected response, the rudder was sufficiently responsive and effective, although only small amounts of sideslips could be applied due to heavy foot forces. Between 0.94 and 0.97 M the lateral control remained satisfactory but the longitudinal control was somewhat touchy. This characteristic was noticeable when small amounts of 'g' were applied or when re-trimming to counteract the slight nose-down trim change which occurs during this range of Mach numbers. It was manifest as over-controlling which was of a mild degree but might make aiming difficult. Slightly heavier stick forces over this range might improve matters. A small amount of buffet was apparent on occasions around these Mach numbers but it was not consistent and its magnitude was small enough to be disregarded. Above 0.97 M the longitudinal sensitivity decreased, control became much more pleasant and accurate flying became easy once more. The nose-down change of trim required about 1 degree of tailplane to trim out, but the stick forces were light and the trim setting was not critical.

High IMN – Flight at supersonic Mach numbers was restricted to gentle manoeuvres using not more than $\frac{1}{3}$ aileron and a maximum 'g' of 3. The maximum Mach number achieved was 1.28 indicated in an estimated 30-degree dive at full throttle from 40,000 ft, the maximum IMN being reached between 25,000 and 30,000 ft. The aircraft was very pleasant to fly up to the permitted limits, the ailerons being responsive and effective and giving an adequate rate of roll for the amount of aileron angle used. The tailplane response was as usual, i.e. a little sluggish but adequate, and there was ample effectiveness for 3 g. The rudder forces were very heavy, permitting only a small amount of pedal movement and having a negligible effect on the aircraft. The stick forces were satisfactory up to 3 g, but it is thought that they may be rather heavy for higher values of 'g'. It remains to be seen just what 'g' will eventually be attainable and also what the drag penalties will be. It may be found inadvisable to use 'g' much in excess of 3, in which case the present stick forces would be satisfactory.

High IAS – The limiting IAS of 600 kts was recorded at various Mach numbers and altitudes. The handling at supersonic Mach numbers is as above. At subsonic Mach numbers 600 kts was reached with about 8,000 rpm. Acceleration to this figure was rapid, and once reached was slow to reduce even when throttled well back. The ailerons were responsive and very effective without being over-sensitive. The tailplane response was less sluggish than at lower speeds but could still not be described as crisp, although this was not found to be any disadvantage. The tailplane was very effective and the control forces were pleasantly light. The 'g' restriction of 3 over 500 knots was reached with light stick forces and could easily be exceeded but it was considered unlikely that heavier stick forces will be necessary, bearing in mind that the design limitation is 7 g. The foot forces were heavy and the small amount of rudder available produced an equally small amount of sideslip. At 400 kts IAS at 2,000 ft a slight buffet commenced at 4 g and a distinct feeling of lightening was apparent although there was no actual pitch-up.

Manoeuvre Boundaries – An attempt was made to investigate the buffet and manoeuvre boundaries as far as the limits would allow in the usual manner, that is by increasing the rate of turn while keeping the Mach number constant. Due to the rapid and considerable drag rise associated with 'g' no satisfactory results were obtained as it was not found possible to steepen the spiral sufficiently rapidly to maintain the Mach number. It was noticed, however, that the low buffet boundary which was a previous feature of the aircraft had been much improved. No buffet could be appreciated above the normal engine vibration in turns up to 4 g at 1.00 IMN and in turns up to 3 g at Mach numbers in excess of 1.0.

The second Boscombe Down assessment thus substantiated the findings of the first preview, but it was clear that the P.1A was nearing its limit and it was unlikely that anything new would be discovered as regards the aircraft's handling characteristics until more thrust was available. In the short term a rudimentary reheat system had been devised for the P.1A that would extend its useful life and provide useful data pending the arrival of the Avon-powered P.1B. One thing it had already achieved, however, was to confound the prophets of doom who, less than a decade before, had considered the so-called 'sound barrier' to be an impenetrable obstacle and therefore too difficult (and costly) to attempt to overcome. In one ill-considered judgement the UK's aeronautical supremacy had been surrendered and a number of pilots were to die as British manufacturers tried to catch up with the achievements of others. But for an inspired design by Petter and his team, it is most likely that Britain would never have produced its own supersonic fighter, but would have been totally reliant on foreign purchases for its air defences.

CHAPTER TWO

Flying to the Limit

The fixed-nozzle reheat system was installed in WG760 towards the end of 1955, and it was flown for the first time in this condition on 31 January 1956. With reheat selected, power was increased to around 9,200 lb s.t. (an increase of approximately 20 per cent), but the use of a fixed nozzle optimized for maximum reheat actually reduced dry thrust to only 5,500 lb s.t. This meant that the loss of an engine after take-off would be extremely serious as there would be insufficient thrust to climb without reheat on the good engine, and at that time the system was not completely reliable. On the plus side the extra thrust allowed the flight envelope to be extended, although increased fuel consumption in reheat cut sortie times even further to around 20 minutes.

Already blessed with an exceptional rate of climb, in reheat WG760 reached 40,000 ft around 3½ minutes after brake release, and speed in level flight at the tropopause was quickly increased to 1.4 M. This improved performance highlighted once again the inadequacies of the aircraft's flight instruments, which were virtually useless immediately after take-off owing to the steep angle of climb. Roland Beamont referred to this problem in one of his trials reports:

> Operation with reheat has confirmed the expected rapid rate of climb and rate of level speed increase. Performance of this order brings into sharp focus the urgent need for improved flight instruments and improved navigational facilities. Even in this power configuration (which is 35 per cent less than that of the P.1B at M=1.00) a climb angle of 45 degrees is developed at M=0.90 from 20,000 ft and at this attitude very little visual reference is available laterally, and none forwards. Of the existing flight instruments:
>
> The 0.8/1.8 Machmeter is so cramped in scale at the subsonic range that accurate climbs with it have proved impossible (and a 1.3 instrument which is satisfactory in this respect has had to be fitted in addition).

The vertical speed indicator is permanently off the scale from take-off.

At the maximum climb rate of 20,000 ft/min developed at 15,000 ft the altimeter rotates so rapidly that unless it is given constant attention the pilot develops a phase-lag of approximately 10,000 ft in reading it.

The ASI reads satisfactorily, but is inadequate for basic climb control owing to the rapidity of the drop-off at constant Mach at these climb rates.

The turn and slip indicator is satisfactory.

Accurate climb patterns are not possible therefore, even under visual conditions, unless a 1.3 Machmeter is fitted in addition to the 1.8 instrument, and even with this addition IF (Instrument Flying) climbs are not practical. For the latter the minimum additional requirement is an effective attitude indicator and a 0.8/1.8 Machmeter with a less cramped subsonic scale.

Navigation of these short-duration, high-performance sorties has already confirmed, if confirmation was in fact needed, that the relatively short delays in VHF communication which occur due to interference and other factors, can result in positioning errors of 20–30 miles in less than 10 minutes from take-off. This order of error can have serious consequences on a sortie planned for 400/400 lb fuel downwind; and for this reason, and as only marginal weather has been experienced in this series, the average fuel after landing has been greater than 450/450 lb.

Instead of the usual test run over the Irish Sea, special permission had been granted for supersonic overland flights in view of the nature of the trials and the fact that fuel was even more critical than it had been before. Every effort was made to prevent built-up areas being affected by sonic booms, but Preston at the start of the run and Appleby at the end were both in the firing line. On the first flight Preston was hit by a 'colossal' boom as the P.1A, already supersonic in the climb, was turned onto course, and on subsequent flights the climb angle had to be steepened even further to stay below 1.0 M until the town had been passed. Appleby was not as fortunate, as it proved to be impossible to amend the flight profiles, and the town continued to be 'boomed' until the end of the trial.

The high-speed runs were extended in 0.05 M stages up to 1.45 M, with checks being made on the aircraft's damping characteristics in pitch, roll and yaw at each test point. Without exception stick displacements in pitch and roll resulted in excellent damping, but as speed was increased it became apparent that directional stability was gradually deteriorating.

In response to left rudder a lurching Dutch roll began, which took longer than before to damp out. In addition, above 1.40 M a high-frequency vibration was felt which was thought to be intake 'buzz'.

By February 1956 the P.1A had been taken to 1.45 M, any increase on this figure being dependent on especially low upper-air temperatures, which would decrease fuel consumption and allow a slightly longer acceleration period. These favourable conditions existed on 24 February, and Beamont watched as the Machmeter crept slowly up to 1.5 M (approximately 1,000 mph). Stability tests were conducted once again with excellent damping in pitch; roll damping was not as good but was considered to be perfectly adequate. Directionally, however, an input of left rudder produced the expected yaw to the left, but this remained after the pedals were released until the aircraft began to lurch to the right, this motion being repeated for 3–4 cycles. At this point Beamont cut the reheat (with 1.53 M indicated) and returned to Warton.

During these high-speed trials supersonic manoeuvring had shown that the P.1A behaved impeccably. An indication of pilot confidence was that stick-free Dutch rolls had been attempted in trimmed 3 g turns at speeds above 1.2 M. Supersonic flight up to 1.4 M was sustained for up to 5 minutes, and turns had been made up to 4 g at 1.30 M and up to 3 g at 1.40 M. To ascertain the effectiveness of the tailplane the stick was pulled fully aft during a level turn at 1.30 M so that the tailplane was at its maximum deflection of -20 degrees. This resulted in a maximum acceleration of 4.2 g with a slight amount of buffet. Such excellent level of control was achieved without the use of autostability.

Although one further flight was made to 1.53 M, the P.1A was never flown to such speeds again, as it had provided all the data required for the P.1B and had confirmed that more fin area was needed if the design requirement of 1.7 M for production aircraft was to be attained with adequate directional stability. Further trials at high IAS (625–675 kts) also highlighted the problem of heat build-up through skin friction. With engines at full power cockpit conditions were adequate with sufficient cooling air being delivered, but when power was reduced in the descent there was a dramatic reduction in the amount of cooling air being admitted to the cockpit and conditions became uncomfortably hot.

In late 1956 WG760 was modified with a cambered leading edge on the outer portion of the wing to improve the aircraft's drag at high subsonic speeds. Although successful, this revised planform only appeared many years later on the Lightning F.6/F.53, F.2A and T.55. With its new wing shape, WG760 was used for stall/spin trials commencing on 4 June 1958.

Like all aircraft with highly swept or delta wings, the P.1A was capable of flying at very high angles of attack, and compared to more conventional aircraft its landing speed was considerably higher than its stall speed. This was owing to the fact that the aircraft's nose-up attitude at touchdown had to be restricted to prevent the tail bumper striking the runway. This occurred at an incidence of around 14.5 degrees, approximately 7 degrees below the stalling angle of attack. Depending on touchdown weight, landing speed was around 140 kts IAS, whereas actual stalling speed using maximum angle of attack was around 110 kts IAS. During the investigations into slow speed flight Roland Beamont had an eventful sortie in WG760 which he described in an article for *Aeroplane Monthly* magazine:

> The schedule called for a slow-down at 20,000 ft, again to the full power with almost full back stick thrust-equals-drag (T=D) point, followed by a gradual reduction of power until either a full stall occurred or lack of elevator trim power allowed the nose to drop and IAS to increase – with the onboard instrumentation recording and the chase Meteor filming.
>
> It was a fine, clear day as the small formation headed north over Blackpool away from the sunglare, and as before the P.1A, nose-high at around 21 degrees AOA (Angle of Attack) reached T=D at 122 kts IAS, with the Meteor wallowing and struggling to keep in station up-sun behind for photography. In my small, but by now very familiar, cockpit everything seemed extremely normal except that at full throttle (max dry) with the nose pointing at the sky we were not going anywhere at all! I eased the stick back to the aft stop and the ASI dropped through 110 kts, the descent rate increased and at 108 kts quite suddenly and very smoothly the P.1A rolled to port.
>
> There was no yaw or buffet, the nose was still high and I felt instinctively that this was an undemanded port roll from the ailerons or from some other configuration-change like a flap asymmetry. But immediate right stick did not help, and as the roll to port continued past the inverted, the nose pitched down and yawed left, and I then came out of my stupor and realized that we were spinning! Taking the planned corrective action I centred the stick progressively (or so I thought), then pushed on outspin (right) rudder, and by half-way round the second full turn I had started to ease the stick forward from neutral – but nothing much happened!
>
> Still with full outspin rudder and now with the stick on the forward stop, the P.1A set off into turn three, but this time the nose pitched down to over-the-vertical from the inverted position – at least it was responding to my forward stick and seemed about to

enter an inverted spin! Two things then began to register. This spin was not really responding to anything I could think of – and we were well below 15,000 ft on the fast-unwinding altimeter, the minimum briefed height for spin recovery after which we were supposed to use the Martin Baker option. Even then I was reluctant to abandon this situation which I had a feeling (later justified) of being partly responsible for. But then the mind cleared and I remembered the only recently installed anti-spin parachute.

Centring the controls, I pulled the spin chute handle and almost immediately there was a jolt, the nose pitched further down and the rolling stopped with the P.1A in a left-banked near-vertical dive. A glance at the ASI showed 120 kts and rising, and I resisted the strong temptation to pull out of the dive (and probably back into 'departure'), while noting with interest the altimeter unwinding swiftly through 9,000 ft. There would also be much lag in this reading, but there was still a margin to spare and so I delayed easing back on the stick until 160 kts, and then recovered to level at 6,500 ft to find the engines still running and no further problems. I jettisoned the spin chute and returned to Warton.

Much was learned from this event, not least that a long period of success in an experimental programme must never be allowed to lead to complacency in the planning of corner-point tests. For example we had apparently planned a potentially critical test point at 10,000 ft lower than our own safety criteria had suggested. Then, although I had absorbed the briefing on recommended recovery action, in the event instead of fully centring the ailerons, the instrumentation and the Meteor's cine camera film confirmed that I had held in 5 degrees of outspin aileron throughout 2½ turns of the spin. Later the P.1B intensive spinning programme revealed that with any outspin aileron applied the Lightning (and the P.1A) would never recover from a spin!

Although the Lightning was never cleared for intentional spinning, Pilot's Notes had to advise those unlucky (or foolish) enough to end up in a spin of what to do. An extensive spinning programme was carried out by Warton's test pilots that involved over 200 spins with various CG loadings and configurations. The Lightning did not display any particularly dangerous characteristics; indeed in many cases the aircraft would recover if the controls were released. However, height loss was considerable, and at least 10,000 ft was needed to come out of an erect spin, with even more height being required for recovery from an inverted spin (see Chapter 11 for a description of the stall/spin characteristics of the Lightning F.6).

CHAPTER THREE

Testing the P.1B

By 1957 the P.1A had reached the limit of its performance and the remainder of the flight envelope would be investigated by the P.1B. This looked much more like the definitive Lightning with its circular nose intake and fixed centrebody, and a large bubble canopy that blended into a fuselage spine used to house various ancillaries, including the iso-propyl-nitrate (Avpin) tanks for the Plessey starter. Owing to the problems experienced on the P.1A, the P.1B featured revised airbrakes that were positioned ahead of the fin. The major advance, however, was the replacement of the Sapphire engines with two Rolls-Royce Avon RA24Rs with a combined thrust in reheat of nearly 30,000 lb, together with revised jet pipes and reheat nozzles.

The first P.1B (XA847) was taken into the air for the first time by Roland Beamont on 4 April 1957, and it was followed by XA853, first flown by English Electric test pilot Desmond de Villiers on 5 September, and XA856 flown by Beamont on 3 January 1958. The progress of the test programme was such that a team from CFE were given clearance to carry out a preview of the P.1B commencing on 17 January 1958. The pilots involved were Wg Cdr E. James of the All Weather Development Squadron (AWDS) and Wg Cdr C.W. Coulthard and Flt Lt P. Carr of AFDS; all flying being carried out from Warton under radar surveillance provided by Boulmer. At the termination of the trial on 4 March, thirteen sorties had been flown in XA847, with a further two in XA856.

Although the P.1B's 'prodigious' performance was appreciated, the fact that it was still some way short of the final production standard tended to inhibit what was meant to be a tactical trial. Compared to the future F.1, XA847 lacked autopilot, autostabilization and a weapons system, and was also deficient in fuel and radio navigation aids. The report that was eventually compiled by CFE was critical in several respects. The Plessey Avpin starter system gave continual trouble and it was exceptional to obtain a first-attempt start. Average time to achieve idling rpm was 33 seconds per engine, and it was necessary to maintain fast idle on the No. 2 engine to give the 54 per cent rpm required to operate the alternator. Foot loads during taxiing were fairly heavy and this could be tiring on long, winding perimeter tracks.

For take-off it was important to align the aircraft correctly, otherwise brake was necessary to correct any directional errors until the rudder became effective at around 100 kts IAS. Take-off run was around 1,000 yards (clean, no flaps), a further 200 yards being needed when taking off with a ventral tank fitted. It was necessary to climb the aircraft after take-off to avoid exceeding the undercarriage limiting speed (250 kts IAS), and it was felt that retraction time (especially the nosewheel) was excessive. Acceleration to the recommended climb speed of 450 kts IAS was rapid and there was no difficulty in holding this speed. At 18,000 ft, however, 0.90 IMN became the climb speed and this was much more difficult to maintain because of the relatively large fore-and-aft stick movements required and the cramped subsonic scale on the Machmeter. Climb attitude for the clean aircraft was around 20 degrees (18 degrees with ventral tank).

At the top of the climb the push-over into level flight required a large stick movement, producing about 0.3 g, and resulted in the pilot's hand obscuring the attitude indicator. Stick force had to be maintained until the tailplane trimmer caught up, otherwise an inadvertent climb resulted. During subsonic handling the ailerons were extremely light and very effective so that constant banked turns were difficult to achieve accurately, even with concentration on the instruments. The rate of roll was very rapid except at low IAS, where coarse application of aileron induced adverse yaw, which led to reduced lateral control until the yaw was corrected by rudder. Below 0.90 IMN and 220 kts IAS control was poor and the aircraft tended to wallow.

During the trial reheat light-up was very unreliable above 30,000 ft and at speeds below 1.0 IMN, so all accelerations had to be carried out at 28,000 ft in maximum cold power up to 1.0 IMN before selecting reheat. Reheat was engaged by opening the throttles to 100 per cent cold thrust, at which point the movement was restricted. A firm push was then required to move the throttles into the reheat range, but once the resistance had been overcome the push force returned to normal. Light-up (when it occurred) was instantaneous and was accompanied by a clearly audible 'thump' from each engine and a sudden surge of power. If all was well the rpm remained at 100 per cent, JPTs stabilized and the nozzle indicators showed fully open (maximum reheat). Acceleration in full reheat was very rapid, and care was needed to maintain level flight as it was easy to climb inadvertently or exceed limiting Mach. Reheat cancellation was effected by throttling back to the minimum reheat stop, lifting a catch below the throttles so as to move them back into the cold thrust range. Engagement and cancellation of reheat was considered to be awkward and jerky and usually resulted in an overshoot beyond the desired throttle setting.

Turns at supersonic speed required complete concentration on the instruments owing to a lack of harmony between the ultra-light ailerons and the disproportionately large stick movements needed for tailplane control. This situation was clearly undesirable as in an actual interception the pilot would not be able to fly accurately and monitor the AI radar at the same time. It was appreciated that an autopilot and autostabilization would improve the situation; indeed, it was felt that they would be essential for the aircraft to be operated effectively. Difficulty was also experienced in achieving certain speeds: 1.30 IMN could not be achieved with 100 per cent cold power but was exceeded with minimum reheat, such was the gap in thrust between the two settings.

The new airbrakes were considered to be relatively ineffective, especially at subsonic speeds, and doubts were expressed as to whether they would be sufficient to cope with the rapid speed alterations that were necessary in the final stages of a blind attack using AI. It was also felt that the variable operation of the airbrakes was unnecessary as maximum extension was invariably required. A phenomenon peculiar to the P.1B was noticed whenever the engines were throttled back at speeds below Mach 1.0. This was 'bleed valve roar', a loud aerodynamic noise which was rather disconcerting for the pilot and would also occur during slight 'g' loadings (0.75 g) in straight flight or in a turn.

For recovery, 0.90 IMN was maintained with airbrakes out, converting to 400 kts IAS below 20,000 ft, although this resulted in an 18-degree nose-down attitude, which was considered to be rather steep, and it was felt that 375 kts IAS was an optimum speed for a QGH pro-cedure. One QGH resulted in breaking out of cloud into moderately heavy rain when forward visibility at 210 kts IAS was found to be nil. In light continuous rain, however, the forward visibility (two miles) was acceptable at circuit speeds. The nose-down attitude in the descent resulted in the fuel gauges under-reading by at least 200 lb per gauge. This error disappeared only when a positive angle of incidence was restored on levelling out.

Visual circuit joining was carried out by running in at 300 kts IAS with about 65 per cent power and breaking into the downwind leg while extending the airbrakes and closing the throttles. Speed fell rapidly to 250 kts IAS, at which point the undercarriage was lowered and power increased to 77 per cent to maintain 220 kts IAS. There was virtually no trim change during undercarriage extension and the main wheels locked down with loud 'clunks', followed after a considerable interval by the nosewheel. With airbrakes still out, the crosswind turn was initiated about one mile downwind of the runway threshold, with flaps being extended prior to the finals turn. With speed now around 190–200 kts IAS, adverse yaw became very noticeable, especially in turbulent conditions. A long, straight and fairly high approach was flown at 75–80 per cent power, allowing the speed to gradually fall off to 170 kts over the threshold. As power response to even small throttle movements was very sensitive, it was best to allow speed to decay gradually in a relatively steep approach. In a low 'drag-in' approach the speed was likely to fall off too early, leading to throttle juggling.

Power was maintained up to the hold-off point (165 kts IAS), when the throttles were closed and the stick pulled right back. After touch-down the stick was moved fully forward to lower the nosewheel and allow the drag chute to be streamed. To prevent the nose rising when the chute deployed the stick was kept hard forward. Even without the use of wheel brakes deceleration with the drag chute was impressive, and the aircraft would be down to taxi speeds by 1,600–1,700 yards. Moderate brake in addition to the braking parachute would stop the aircraft in 1,100–1,200 yards. For a missed approach, the overshoot was straightforward and could be carried out using 90 per cent power with airbrakes out.

Despite its criticism in certain areas, the CFE team expressed its grati-fication that the performance of the P.1B was well up to expectations, and with regard to the requirements in speed, climb and acceleration it promised to be capable of Mach 2.0 in service. Owing to limitations at the time, operational ceiling could not be investigated fully, but it appeared highly probable that the requirement (55,000 ft) would be exceeded too. From the point of view of pure aerodynamic performance, the P.1B was likely to have a handsome superiority over the contempo-rary bomber threat posed by the subsonic Tu-16 Badger operating at altitudes a little below 50,000 ft. Although the aircraft was not difficult to fly, it kept an experienced fighter pilot very busy throughout simu-lated operational missions right up to the recovery phase. During the trial there was a good example of the high levels of piloting ability that would be needed with the Lightning. An interception profile was launched when cloud was continuous from 800 to 30,000 ft. After take-off a reciprocal turn was required, and this was begun before climbing speed was reached and was carried out using bank angles between 45 and 60 degrees. Because of the very high rate of climb, the need to push-over into level flight at 30,000 ft occurred before the 180-degree turn after take-off had been completed.

At the time of the CFE trial, limiting speeds were 1.7 IMN (clean) and 1.5 IMN (ventral), but it was obvious that the aircraft was capable of a lot more. Although the P.1B was to pioneer the first of the Lightning's fin enlargements to maintain directional stability at high speed, without the destabilizing effect of nose-mounted missiles it was considered that the top end of the speed range could be explored further without waiting for the taller fin. In the face of a distinct lack of interest from official circles, English Electric pressed ahead with handling and performance tests at higher speeds, and by November 1958 the P.1B had been flown at Mach 1.92. Particular attention was given to the possibility of intake 'buzz' at these speeds and also any thermal stress problems associated with high ram air temperatures in excess of 100° C.

It was clear that the magic figure of Mach 2.00 was attainable, and on 25 November 1958 the upper air conditions were particularly favourable, with a high tropopause and a temperature of –70° C at 40,000 ft. There would never be a better opportunity to achieve the milestone of flight at twice the speed of sound, and English Electric was well aware of the publicity that such an achievement would bring. The pilot, as ever, was Roland Beamont, who achieved Mach 2.00 with the aircraft still accelerating over the Irish Sea.

Although the P.1B was capable of performance levels well in excess of the service requirement, like its immediate predecessor it suffered from a chronic shortage of internal fuel (574 gallons usable). Although it could safely explore the speed range up to Mach 1.7, thanks to efficiencies derived from its variable nozzle reheat system and the increased thrust of its Avon RA24Rs, accelerations above this Mach number meant that fuel reserves were virtually non-existent and the recovery had to be right first time, as there was often not enough fuel left for an overshoot following a missed approach. Later, XA847 appeared with an enlarged ventral tank, which was the forerunner of the installation used on the F.2A/F.6. It was also fitted with the larger 'Stage 2' fin, and later tested a revised fin with dorsal fillet to maintain directional stability when carrying two Red Top missiles. This design was soon dropped, however, in favour of the familiar 'square-topped' fin first seen on the Lightning F.3.

It is difficult to overestimate the significance of the P.1B to the British aircraft industry. Not only had it been flown to Mach 2.00 at a time when very few other projects in the world had achieved such a feat, but it had done so with performance to spare, as there was still an excess of thrust over drag at this speed. Very few problems had been experienced, and stability and control were such that gentle manoeuvres could be flown at Mach 2.00 without autostabilization. To those working on the Lightning programme it was obvious that the aircraft had tremendous potential and was let down only by lack of fuel and its rather limited armament. Having already proved its worth courtesy of the P.1A/P.1B, the Lightning was crying out to be developed so that it could achieve its full potential. Unfortunately it was to get precious little, thanks to an inept defence policy which had decreed that manned interceptors were no longer required (missiles being preferred instead) and a parsimonious Treasury.

CHAPTER FOUR

Lightning F.1 Service Release Handling Trials

In terms of the Lightning's development, Boscombe Down took centre stage between September 1959 and May 1960 as the final handling trials were carried out prior to CA release and squadron service. In this period nine aircraft (in varying states of modification) passed through the establishment, each allotted a particular task, as follows:

XA853	Split flaps + small fin	Engine handling, including the effect of gun firing on engine behaviour
XG307	Split flaps + large fin	Demonstration of autostabilizer malfunctions
XG308	Split flaps + large fin	Assessment of stability and control, and engine behaviour
XG310	Split flaps + small fin	Assessment of auto ILS
XG313	Plain flaps + large fin	Assessment of plain flaps and of stability and control at more extreme CG positions
XG325	Plain flaps + large fin	Assessment of 'manual' ILS and plain flaps
XG331	Plain flaps + large fin	Assessment of stability and control, and engine handling on an aircraft approaching production standard

| XG337 | Plain flaps + large fin | Demonstration of certain emergency flight conditions |
| XM134 | Plain flaps + large fin | Assessment of stability and control, and engine handling of production aircraft |

A new aerodynamic feature was the use of plain flaps on later development batch and production aircraft instead of split flaps as used previously. In addition most aircraft were by now fitted with the enlarged Stage 2 fin. Flying limits during the test period varied from aircraft to aircraft and in some instances were subject to change. In general they were as follows:

Condition	Max speed (kts IAS)	Max IMN
Experimental flying	700 (675 rolling)	1.7 (1.5 with ventral tank, 1.3 with ventral tank and missiles)
Airbrakes out	650	1.4 (1.2 rolling)
Flaps down	250	–
Undercarriage down	250	–

Maximum take-off weight was 31,700 lb (34,000 lb overload), and the minimum flying speed was 135 kts IAS. Rolling manoeuvres were the subject of a number of restrictions except during take-off and landing, and flight within the circuit. Rolls up to 90 degrees at speeds up to 550 kts IAS/1.7 M and 4 g (or the onset of buffet) were limited to half aileron. Rolls up to 180 degrees were also to be half aileron, but with a reduced load factor of 2 g. At speeds above 550 kts IAS co-ordinated turns using low rates of roll only were permitted, and during normal accelerations of less than 1 g only minimum use of aileron could be used at any speed. These limits had been imposed following the loss of T.4 XL628 (see Chapter 12), but the Lightning proved to be easy to handle even without autostabilization, and it was considered that service pilots would have no difficulty in converting from subsonic types. However, A&AEE reported unfavourably on the cockpit layout, particularly the restricted space that meant that the large number of instruments and switches associated with the aircraft's many systems resulted in an over-complicated layout.

Considering the aircraft's speed range and the heights that were attainable, it was considered that English Electric had done a fine job with the flying controls, the only quibble being the stick to tailplane gearing, which it was felt could be improved. Take-off and landing was also straightforward on production aircraft with plain flaps. The transonic characteristics were found to be innocuous, and the small and gentle nose-down pitch still remained when passing from subsonic to supersonic conditions. This situation was naturally reversed when decelerating, the nose-up pitch being accentuated under applied 'g' conditions, although it could readily be kept to within ½–1 g. Slight transonic buffet was also noted at about 0.98–0.99 M (apparently attributable to the ventral tank) but was of little significance.

At supersonic speeds up to 1.4 M, static stability became slightly negative (except in the clean configuration), but this characteristic did not cause any handling difficulties or criticism. Although dynamic stability without the use of autostabilizers was adequate for general flying, it was thought that some difficulties would be encountered with weapon aiming at higher altitudes, particularly during a guns attack. Use of autostabilizers produced a marked improvement in damping characteristics without introducing any adverse effects on general handling qualities.

With regard to longitudinal stability, tailplane control was considered adequate, even in such extreme conditions as flying without hydraulic 'feel' or at the extended aft CG position as would occur if the ventral tank failed to transfer its fuel. Plain flaps as fitted to late development batch and production aircraft also brought about a marked improvement in tailplane response during the round-out on landing. Fuselage incidence during the approach was reduced (by about 2 degrees), allowing a better forward view, and the position of the control column was further forward, giving more scope for back stick at the flare.

A certain amount of negative static stability was encountered at supersonic speeds, pilots being conscious of a reversal of stick movement around 1.3–1.4 M, although it was not serious enough to cause any embarrassment in simulated operational sorties and could be trimmed out. This was achieved by adjusting the electrically operated trimmer switches on top of the control column. Longitudinal trimming was a little on the slow side, but in one sense this was no bad thing as it lessened the risk of runaway trim.

Tailplane forces were regarded as being somewhat light at low altitudes with an aft CG position and rather heavy at high altitude with a forward CG. However, even with a full ventral tank and hydraulic 'feel' switched off, leaving just the residual spring to provide control 'feel', the forces were not so light as to be dangerous. Some criticism was made of the stick/tailplane gearing in that some negative tailplane movement (and hence manoeuvring capacity) could easily be lost as the stick came up against the pilot's body. This fault was accentuated at the more forward CG positions and applied particularly to supersonic flight at high altitude. At the time of the trial English Electric was working towards a modification that reduced stick travel by about 15 degrees and increased the gearing at all tailplane deflections.

Aileron control was considered satisfactory in both response and the amount of force required. The only doubt appeared to be whether the desired rate of roll could be achieved in turbulent approach conditions. Rudder control was rated as adequate for the limited use demanded in a high-speed aircraft. It became effective for directional control at an early stage in the take-off run (around 50–60 kts) and it was not the limiting factor in crosswind landings. Although successful landings were made on split-flap aircraft in crosswind components up to 30 knots and on plain-flap aircraft in crosswinds up to 24 knots, severe tyre scuffing was experienced to the point where the tyres had to be replaced. The crosswind limits as proposed for release to service varied with respect to runway condition: 25 kts (dry), 20 kts (wet), 15 kts (flooded).

In the interests of structural strength the rudder control forces had been made to increase with increased airspeed. Pedal forces in the order of 100 lb per degree of rudder deflection were measured at speeds just over 600 kts IAS. During the trial it was also noticeable that aircraft with the fin and rudder of increased area did not show any adverse aileron yaw as had been experienced on those machines fitted with the original-sized unit. The range of rudder trimming proved to be only just adequate owing to variations in directional trim with Mach number. English Electric had a number of theories to explain this, including misalignment of the Firestreak missiles and a slight asymmetry of engine thrust caused by malfunctioning of the reheat nozzles.

Particular attention was paid to the airbrakes as A&AEE had reported unfavourably on these in the past. Extension of the airbrakes within the permitted limit of 650 kts/1.4 IMN caused only slight buffeting and negligible change in trim. At the worst conditions of limiting airspeed and limiting Mach number, a transient nose-down pitch change equivalent to about 1 g was experienced stick free, but when the pilot was flying with his hand on the control column the disturbance was automatically corrected and the nose-down moment was hardly noticed. However, the lack of effectiveness noted previously was still apparent, particularly in the interception phase and when in the circuit. A second major criticism of the airbrakes was the limitation of 1.4 IMN in straight flight and 1.2 IMN in rolling flight. The lack of speed control at higher

Mach numbers by other than engine throttling or changes in flight attitude was regretted, but accepted, albeit reluctantly.

Trim changes with flap and undercarriage operation were small, although some lateral rocking was noted during undercarriage retraction through non-symmetric operation. There was also a reduction in the retraction time of the nosewheel compared with previous aircraft. This had led to problems in that the undercarriage limit speed was liable to be exceeded, but this criticism no longer applied when both services hydraulic pumps were functioning correctly.

Even without autostabilization pitch damping was excellent at high supersonic speeds at medium to high altitudes. Yaw and roll damping was not up to the same standard, but was still acceptable. With auto-stabilizers functioning there was a marked increase in the aircraft's damping, which enhanced its handling and sighting qualities. This improvement was most noticeable in the pitching sense at supersonic speeds and in the lateral sense at all airspeeds, including the approach to land. In the latter condition the autostabilizer resulted in an appreciable improvement in turbulent air with a significant reduction in the peak rates of roll encountered. From both qualitative and quantitative points of view the system was highly regarded, and at no time did a pilot feel that the autostabilization was trying to oppose his normal control inputs.

Around twenty approaches were flown with XG325 under manual ILS conditions. The usual technique was to fly downwind at about 300 kts IAS at 3,000 ft before turning crosswind at ten miles downwind with engines throttled and airbrakes extended. Height and speed were then reduced and undercarriage extended at 240 kts IAS at 2,000 ft. In the first few approaches crosswind heading was maintained until the localizer needle showed the beginning of beam interception, but this was found to lead to an overshoot and subsequent oscillation about the localizer beam. To overcome this tendency a turn was made onto the localizer around 1½ miles offset from the beam, the final approach pattern consisting of turning onto a heading approximately 50 degrees to runway heading. It then proved possible to turn onto the localizer beam from this angle when the needle began to move without any further corrections having to be made. Speed was maintained at 200 kts IAS to the glidepath interception, at which point flaps were extended and the engines throttled further. Lowering of the flaps caused the aircraft to rise above the glidepath, but subsequent behaviour was satisfactory with good ILS indicator response. XG310 was used for auto-ILS assessment. Unacceptable height loss was experienced (up to 1,000 ft/min on the VSI) following the engagement of the autopilot, leading to the aircraft being returned to English Electric for rectification work, after which there was a considerable improvement.

A limited amount of performance testing had been intended for the Boscombe Down trial, but because of slippage of the Lightning programme this was not possible. English Electric figures were quoted instead, but like most manufacturers' assessments they tended to flatter the company product somewhat and could not be regarded as an accurate assessment, except under ideal conditions. With a take-off weight of 34,000 lb, flaps up and maximum thrust without reheat, English Electric calculated a runway length to reach a height of 50 ft as 4,100 ft; however, A&AEE though that 5,000 ft would be a more realistic figure. Similarly English Electric calculated that a Lightning could be stopped within 4,880 ft on a wet runway with a landing weight of 29,000 lb, airbrakes extended and braking parachute deployed, whereas A&AEE thought that 5,600 ft was more representative. Even so, this would (in theory) not be a problem, as once in service Lightnings would be operating from 7,500 ft runways to allow for the extreme conditions of brake parachute failure, zero wind and a flooded runway.

In its conclusion the A&AEE report commented on the Lightning as follows:

> Within the limits of the present assessment the handling characteristics of the aircraft have been found generally to be excellent. The dynamic stability without autostabilization throughout the flight envelope had been found to be of a high order and autostabilization is not required for reasons of flight safety. It does, however, augment the dynamic stability to the level desirable for weapon aiming and materially improves the aircraft's behaviour in turbulent conditions, being particularly helpful on the approach. Generally also the performance had been shown to meet the Specification requirements with reservations in the take-off performance, which, however, is regarded as in no way critical. Engine handling had been developed to an acceptable standard for initial release but further testing of the fuel control units of the Avon 210s is required before this aspect can be regarded as resolved for general production.

CHAPTER FIVE

Lightning F.1 at CFE

As the Lightning was continuing its service release handling trials at A&AEE, Boscombe Down, several development batch and F.1 machines were delivered to AFDS at Coltishall commanded by Wg Cdr David Simmons AFC.

I took command of AFDS at Coltishall on 29 December 1959. The squadron had just taken delivery of its first development batch Lightning, serial XG334 as a Christmas present. We belonged to CFE at West Raynham under the command of Air Commodore Hugh Edwards VC CB CBE DSO DFC, and later of Air Commodore Geoffrey Millington CB CBE DFC. The squadron had deployed to Coltishall because of the longer runway needed to accommodate Lightnings. When the runway there was ribbed to improve traction we deployed temporarily to Leconfield. Of course there was no trainer version at that time, but we had two very good simulators at Coltishall. My first flight in Lightning XG335 was on 14 March 1960. My logbook entry reads – 'Trial 314, Flt plan No. 1, 1.3 Mach indicated'.

We built up to four Lightning aircraft by July 1960. We celebrated by getting all of them in the air together for a photo call on 11 July. We were in echelon starboard at low level when No. 4, Flt Lt (later AC) Ken Goodwin, called that he had an engine fire warning. I told him to hang on in for the photo if he could before he broke off and returned to base. This indicated an attitude of mind induced by frequent spurious warnings of engine or reheat systems with flashing red lights and clanging in the headphones that resulted in several aborts and single engine landings. Eventually manufacturing swarf in the Graviner switches was thought to be to blame.

We also had hydraulic troubles. Two entries in my logbook for 28 June 1960 read: 'Lightning XM135, Trial 314, Flt plan 32, nose-wheel u/s, 30 minutes', and 'Lightning XM136, Flt plan 23, nosewheel u/s, 15 minutes, night'. The most memorable incident, however, was when I was called to the tower one night. Flt Lt (later AVM) Peter Collins couldn't get one leg of his undercarriage down and was running short of fuel in the circuit. It had already been determined that such a wheels-up landing would be very dangerous. I told him to head to the coast and eject out to sea. On his way there, after several more attempts and simultaneous application of 'g', he got three greens. He landed at Coltishall with pints to spare and was towed from the runway.

As the Lightning was capable of operating at heights far in excess of any previous RAF fighter, pilots had to undergo specialist training before being allowed to fly the aircraft to the extremes of its performance envelope. On successful completion a certificate was presented, that for David Simmons being as follows:

RAF Institute of Aviation Medicine – RAF Farnborough

Aeromedical Training – W/C D.C.H. Simmons 123016

This officer has successfully completed the training programme as laid down in I.A.M. Training Memorandum No. 20 in the use of the pressure helmet (BWT), pressure jerkin, anti-G suit system. In this training he was rapidly decompressed from a simulated altitude of 27,000 ft to 60,000 ft. The duration of the exposure at 60,000 ft was one minute and this was followed by descent to 40,000 ft at 10,000 ft per minute.

Training Period – 19–22 April 1960

Signed S/L J. Ernsting – Specialist in Aviation Physiology – 25/4/60

Apart from a bad case of freckles on his chest and shoulders, Simmons survived the experience in A1 condition!

The first phase of the Lightning trial conducted by AFDS involved the interception of targets operating at 0.85 M between 36,000 and 45,000 ft and was completed by July 1960. Phase 2 began two months later, the main aim being to extend the investigation in terms of height and speed, and build up knowledge of operating the Lightning at supersonic speeds. Progress officer for the trial was Sqn Ldr H. Harrison, with Sqn Ldrs E.F. Babst and R.S. Langton, together with Flt Lts D.I. Evans, P.S. Collins and W.B.G. Hopkins, as project officers.

The trial began on 12 September 1960 and continued until 2 March 1961, by which time 129 hours had been flown in 173 sorties. In all, 137 sorties were classed as having been effective, a success rate of 79 per cent. However, the rate of progress was relatively slow owing to one, and sometimes two, aircraft being laid up for modifications by contractor's working parties, and by unserviceability. The most serious problems affected XM163, which was grounded for over two months while an undercarriage defect was investigated, and XM138, which was damaged Cat 4 because of a hot gas leak after landing (see Chapter 12). Other difficulties included hydraulics, engines and jet pipes and electrical systems, with persistent AC failures. All in all, the defect rate with the F.1 was as bad as it had been with the development-batch aircraft, and it was equally expensive to maintain in terms of maintenance man-hours. The test schedule was also affected by the fact that the Lightnings also had to act as supersonic targets owing to a lack of other types capable of this level of performance. On a more positive note, the AI.23 radar showed some long periods of serviceability once it had settled down after being disturbed.

The findings of Phase 1 of the trial were confirmed in that the loiter capability of the Lightning operating against a target with a speed of 0.85 M was around 10 minutes at a radius of action of 180 nm. The loiter had to be carried out in the height bracket 30,000–38,000 ft to minimize the use of fuel. Flight below 30,000 ft led to a sharp increase in fuel consumption (it also raised the height difference between fighter and target to unacceptable levels), and flight above 38,000 ft required the use of reheat to maintain height and speed. Acceleration from the loitering speed also took longer to achieve. Performance was within 5 per cent of optimum when flying between 30,000 and 38,000 ft, but care had to be taken as the Lightning's loiter speed coincided with significant altimeter pressure errors, and allowance had to be made for this. In the most extreme case at 1.02 M the discrepancy was in the order of 1,700 ft. This was because of shock wave movement and sudden changes in pressure distribution about the static vents in the pitot head, the error disappearing in the form of an altimeter jump on accelerating past 1.02 M.

For reasons of fuel economy and to employ supersonic speed to best advantage, the F.1 had to be climbed in cold power to the 30,000–38,000 ft height bracket and then cruised, accelerated and turned to intercept before its excess speed potential could be used for overtake or for an energy climb. Unlike all previous service fighters which climbed directly to their operating altitudes, the Lightning had to employ this stepped climb technique regardless of target altitude and regardless of whether it was required to loiter or not. When engaging a subsonic target below 45,000 ft it was not necessary to accelerate to supersonic speed except to eliminate errors induced by inaccurate ground control or poor B-scope interpretation. Excessive use of reheat only served to increase the rate of fuel consumption. It also resulted in the Lightning travelling faster round a larger radius of attack, thereby reducing loiter time and radius of action.

The Lightning F.1 also proved to be fully capable of intercepting subsonic targets above 45,000 ft under close or loose radar control. A target flying at 0.85 M at 50,000 ft could be intercepted subsonically if GCI control was sufficiently precise, but a much wider range of target conditions could be met if the Lightning accelerated to low supersonic speeds on AI contact. Owing to a lack of suitable targets, it was not possible to carry out interceptions above 50,000 ft, although it was felt that the Lightning would be successful against subsonic targets operating up to 60,000 ft by using energy climb techniques.

As the latest intelligence estimate was that a threat existed to 1.2 M and 50,000 ft, interceptions were carried out on other Lightnings simulating this type of attack profile. One of the difficulties experienced was that the launch speed of the Firestreak air-to-air missile was then restricted to 1.3 M, which did not allow much room for error. To stand any chance of success against supersonic targets it was found that the interceptor's speed had to at least match that of the incoming aircraft by the time of the attack-phase turn at the tropopause. The acceleration of the Lightning was critical and had to be started when target range was at least 65 nm, putting the onus on the ground controllers to inform the pilot at the appropriate time.

The attack-phase turn also had to be flown accurately as the high speed of both fighter and target resulted in the manoeuvre being carried out at considerable slant range. The turn was usually made level within the loiter-height bracket, and below the 2 g manoeuvre thrust boundary. An energy climb was then employed after roll-out to take out part of the height difference, the 'snap-up' capability of the Firestreak missile being used to nullify the remainder. Although in theory Firestreak could take out another 7,000 ft, in order to retain the best guarantee of success against a manoeuvring target the fighter had to be within the target's 15-degree tail cone before releasing. This limited the height difference at missile release to about 3,000 ft. One particular difficulty experienced during interceptions in this part of the trial was the frequent toppling of the target indicator gyro. The effect of this was to deny the pilot all the advantages of a computed approach path at a critical stage of the attack until the sight could be re-erected by switching the master armament switch off and then on again.

Interceptions were also made against supersonic targets under loose ground control. Provided that the instruction to begin the acceleration was given at the correct time the Lightning was likely to reach an adequate speed to intercept a 1.2 M target, although this presupposed achieving AI contact at about 25 nm range so that the fighter could begin its attack-phase turn. However, a successful interception still depended on the target showing an angle off of 30 degrees or more on initial contact. In the case of a mass raid it would also be difficult to assess on the B-scope which specific target had the height and speed performance that the Lightning was attempting to match. When all of these variables were added together, it was considered that the chances of achieving a successful interception of a supersonic target were slight when given only loose control.

The AFDS trial also reported on the difference in climb and acceleration performance of the Lightning when air temperatures were colder than standard ICAN conditions. The following figures show a marked variation in time and fuel used to perform different aspects of the interception procedure:

Climb to 36,000 ft – Max cold power

Tropopause temp (°C)	Time (min/sec)	Distance (nm)	Fuel used (lb)
-66.5	3.30	24.5	1,150
-56.5	3.45	27	1,200
-46.5	4.05	30	1,250

Acceleration 0.87–1.6 M at 36,000 ft

Tropopause temp (°C)	Time (min/sec)	Distance (nm)	Fuel used (lb)
-66.5	2.20	25	1,050
-56.5	2.40	31	1,200
-46.5	3.20	41	1,500

Tests were also carried out to determine the Lightning F.1's ceiling and rate of acceleration at altitude carrying a ventral tank and two Firestreak missiles. During subsonic climbs in maximum cold power the rate of climb had fallen to 500 ft/min at 45,000 ft, by which time 1,500 lb of fuel had been used. The full use of reheat from 25,000 ft increased the aircraft's ceiling to 50,000 ft. However, this involved a large fuel penalty as an additional 600 lb of fuel was used to reach this height. Absolute ceiling was measured at 54,000 ft. To obtain altitudes above this thrust boundary figure required the use of energy climb techniques.

The level of acceleration performance also fell away rapidly at altitude. At 30,000 ft the Lightning accelerated from 0.9 M to 1.6 M in 1 minute 55 seconds, using 1,075 lb of fuel in the process. When the same exercise was tried at 45,000 ft, it took 6 minutes 55 seconds and used 1,950 lb of fuel. Unless the upper air temperatures were particularly favourable, it was considered unlikely that the Lightning F.1 would be able to accelerate beyond Mach 1.0 in level flight at heights much above 45,000 ft.

Another critical aspect of the Lightning's performance was the 2 g manoeuvre thrust boundary. This figure was reached at 38,000 ft, and any manoeuvring in excess of this boundary resulting in large losses of speed and energy climb potential. For this reason it was recommended that all manoeuvring during the interception be carried out below the 2 g boundary, i.e. below 38,000 ft.

As a result of the trials various intercept profiles were recommended by AFDS for different threats. Assuming a gate position (loiter orbit) 90 nm from the airfield and a fuel state on landing of 800/800 lb, the Lightning needed to be vectored down the lane when the raid entered UK radar cover at around 240 nm. Interception ranges for subsonic targets averaged 155–160 nm from base if the Lightning was vectored from the gate position on initial GCI contact, whereas for a supersonic target cruising at 1.2 M the interception range was a little less, at 145–150 nm (see Figure 1). There were an almost infinite number of permutations, however, as a result of variations in loiter and the amount of time spent in reheat. As an example, a reduction of one minute in loiter time allowed an additional 1½ minutes of cruise and an extra 6 nm on radius of action, whereas each extra minute spent in full reheat reduced loiter time by 4 minutes or radius of action by 24 nm.

A year after completing its tactical trial of the Lightning F.1, AFDS began an evaluation of the Lightning/Firestreak combination in March 1961 that involved a total of seventeen missiles being fired at Meteor U.16 and Jindivik targets. The aircraft used were XM137 and XM163, the detachment being temporarily attached to 'A' Squadron of A&AEE at Boscombe Down. All firings were carried out over the Aberporth range off the Welsh coast near Cardigan. Missiles were fired over a wide range of conditions as follows:

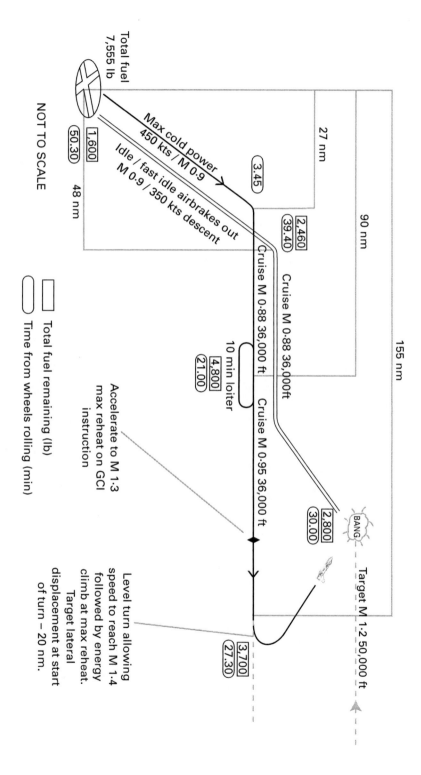

Total fuel
7,555 lb

NOT TO SCALE

27 nm

90 nm

155 nm

Max cold power
450 kts / M 0.9

Idle / fast idle airbrakes out
M 0.9 / 350 kts descent

[3.45]

[50.30]

[1,600]

48 nm

[2,460]
[39.40]

Cruise M 0.88 36,000 ft

Cruise M 0.88 36,000ft

10 min loiter

[4,800]
[21.00]

Cruise M 0.95 36,000 ft

Accelerate to M 1.3
max reheat on GCI
instruction

[2,800]
[30.00]

BANG

Target M 1·2 50,000 ft

Level turn allowing
speed to reach M 1·4
followed by energy
climb at max reheat.
Target lateral
displacement at start
of turn – 20 nm.

[3,700]
[27.30]

Total fuel remaining (lb)

Time from wheels rolling (min)

Fig. 1   Loose Control – Reheat – Supersonic Target

	Minimum	Maximum
Fighter speed	280 kts IAS	650 kts IAS
Fighter Mach	0.62 M	1.68M
Normal acceleration (fighter)	+1 g	+4 g
Fighter altitude	15,000 ft	52,000 ft
Firing range	1,621 yd	6,789 yd
Target altitude	15,000 ft	55,000 ft
Target Mach	0.7 M	0.8 M

During a previous trial with the Firestreak-armed Javelin a harmonization error had been discovered, so this was the first aspect of missile performance to be checked with the Lightning. The error with the Javelin had manifested itself as a jump in the missile eye at the instant the missile went from scan to lock. Several simulated firings were made with telemetry installed to measure eye movement, and the Lightning/Firestreak combination showed a marked improvement.

During the trials no lateral or longitudinal stability problems were encountered, all out-of-trim forces being in the directional sense. A mild oscillation occurred in yaw when the missile was fired at speeds up to 1.3 M/500 kts IAS, and this was amplified when two missiles were fired in sequence as the firing interval and the aircraft's yaw period were in harmony. At 1.5 M/550 kts IAS $^2/_3$ rudder trim was required to trim out the asymmetry caused by single missile carriage, and at 1.7 M/650 kts IAS an estimated 40 lb rudder force was needed to restore trim. In all cases where an oscillation in yaw was experienced, it was quickly damped and presented no problem. However, the situation became a little more marginal during one particular flight, when 3 g was applied at 1.7 M, resulting in a sideslip of approximately 10 degrees. Normally the missile launched 1–2 seconds after the firing trigger was pressed and was characterized by a loud 'tearing' noise from the rocket motor.

Launch rate during the evaluation programme was 49 per cent. Some aborts were caused by instrumentation, and some because either the Lightning or the target was not in the desired position. If these aborts are discounted the launch rate was 71 per cent, which was considered very satisfactory, especially as on all but one sortie only one missile was carried. Missile stability was excellent about all three axes; when oscillation did occur it damped out within a few cycles and did not have any effect on guidance or range. Larger dispersions caused by firing under high 'g' loadings were also quickly damped out. Of the seventeen missiles fired, six were direct hits and seven were near misses, an excellent success rate considering the wide variety of launch conditions.

The overall conclusion was that the Lightning/Firestreak weapon system worked encouragingly well, particularly as a fighter v. fighter weapon, since it was possible to fire the missile when the launch aircraft was pulling up to 4 g. To quote the AFDS report, 'This was considered impossible before [the trial] and, incidentally, still is by others possessing similar weapons.' No incompatibility was detected in aircraft and missile.

CHAPTER SIX

Lightning F.1 Cockpit Analysis

T he closer you get to a Lightning, the more you appreciate that it is a big aircraft. The mid-set wing is just over seven feet from the ground, a height that proved to be ideal for spectators to shelter under at air displays when it rained! The depth of the Lightning fuselage, with its vertically staggered engines, means that the pilot's eye level, at approximately twelve feet above the ground, is higher than most other single-seat fighters. The cockpit, however, is snug, to say the least, and one can be forgiven for thinking that the pilot's working environment was only considered as an afterthought when everything else had been allocated its own place.

The lack of space and layout of the P.1B cockpit had been the subject of considerable debate and no little criticism by Boscombe Down. In an assessment of XA847 it was felt that the cockpit was extremely cramped and in need of a complete redesign before production aircraft began to roll off the assembly line. A&AEE even went so far as to suggest a revised forward fuselage of increased width, but failing this (which was a non-starter because of production considerations) there was an urgent requirement for a rationalization of the large number of switches and indicators, and a redesign of the side consoles. The location of certain levers also left something to be desired, in particular the positioning of the undercarriage selection lever next to the cockpit pressurization lever. By the time the Lightning entered service there had been a considerable improvement in cockpit layout, and it is proposed to take a closer look at the principal features of the F.1/F.1A cockpit.

MARTIN BAKER MK.4BS EJECTION SEAT

Of particular interest to the first-time Lightning pilot was his means of vacating the aircraft in emergency – the Martin Baker Mk.4BS lightweight ejection seat. In theory this seat could be used successfully from ground level, assuming a speed greater than 90 knots, although 250 knots was recommended if at all possible. It came with a back-type parachute with safety harness and a personal survival pack, and was normally activated by a face-screen firing handle above the pilot's head. A secondary firing handle was located on the leading edge of the seat pan if for any reason it was impossible to use the face-screen handle. On the ground both firing handles were de-activated by safety pins with red warning discs attached, these being removed before flight to make the seat 'live' and stowed in the starboard console.

The Mk.4BS seat incorporated a number of advanced features, including a time delay mechanism, incorporating a barostatic control which delayed the opening of the parachute and separation of the pilot from the seat when the ejection was made at high altitude. There was also an automatic 'g' switch fitted on the time delay mechanism which delayed the opening of the parachute if a pilot had been forced to leave his aircraft at high speed. On ejection the pilot's legs were pulled in towards the seat base by automatic leg-restraining gear. On the starboard side of the seat pan a personal equipment connector provided the connection of the following services: main and emergency oxygen, tel/mic lead, air-ventilated suit and anti-g trousers. Forward of this was a seat adjustment switch and to the rear an emergency oxygen control. On the port side of the seat was the harness 'go-forward' lever and a manual release for the harness and leg-restraining gear.

To eject the seat from the aircraft, the pilot grasped the face-screen firing handle with both hands, knuckles facing outwards and elbows close together, and pulled the handle downward. This action jettisoned the canopy and commenced the ejection sequence. The leg-restraining gear then secured the pilot's legs to the forward face of the seat pan and as the seat left the aircraft his face mask was supplied with oxygen from the emergency cylinder. A static line then disengaged the 'aircraft portion' of his personal equipment connector. Half a second after ejection the drogue gun fired, the drogues (when fully developed) retarding and stabilizing the seat in a convenient attitude for separation.

If the ejection had taken place above 10,000 ft, a barostat prevented operation of the time-delay mechanism until this height had been reached, thus enabling the pilot to make a rapid controlled descent to an altitude where emergency oxygen could be dispensed with. After release by the 'g' switch and barostat, the time-delay mechanism simultaneously freed harness, parachute, leg-restraining gear and the 'man portion' of the personal equipment connector from attachment to the seat. All being well, the parachute then developed and lifted the pilot from the seat. In certain emergency situations (i.e. failure of the nosewheel to extend prior to landing) it was recommended that the canopy be jettisoned. This could be accomplished without seat ejection by pulling a yellow and black striped spade-grip handle situated between the ejection seat and the port console.

MAIN FLIGHT INSTRUMENTS

Once safely settled into his seat the pilot was confronted by the main instrument panel. Information for the main flight instruments came from a Master Reference Gyro (MRG), which consisted of a gimballed platform containing vertical and azimuth gyros. This fed electrical signals through 360 degrees in roll, pitch and azimuth, pitch and bank angles being presented on an attitude indicator and heading by the heading indicator which formed part of the Mk.5 FT compass. Both instruments featured OFF flags that were electrically actuated from the MRG and warned of malfunction. On start-up these flags would normally have disappeared from view within 20 seconds of setting the instrument master switch to ON, indicating that the gyros were running at effective speed with the amplifiers warmed up. A switch on the main instrument panel controlled the erection rate of the MRG vertical gyro. In the NORMAL setting erection rate was 3 degrees/min, but if errors were evident, the switch could be adjusted to FAST ERECTION, in which case the erection rate was increased to 17 degrees/min.

The Type F1M Attitude Indicator was a servo-operated roller-blind display unit controlled by the vertical gyro of the MRG. The roller blind was divided laterally into two sections, one white, representing the sky, and the other black, representing the earth, the junction between the two being the horizon. The roller blind was free to rotate through 360 degrees in roll and it wound up or down – with reference to the face of the instruments – to denote pitch. At high angles of climb or dive, a zenith or nadir star respectively was visible on the blind, these stars having a long tail which pointed towards the horizon when this was not visible on the display. Looping manoeuvres which passed through the zenith or nadir resulted in a rapid rotation of the blind through 180 degrees as each of the two points was reached.

Angle of pitch could be measured by the relationship of the horizon or stars to the scale on the cover glass. Two concentric circles marked on the glass indicated 20 degrees (inner circle) and 40 degrees (outer circle), while small marks appropriately spaced on the vertical centre line denoted 10, 30 and 50 degrees. Bank angles were read by the bank pointer on the blind carriage against fixed references at 10, 20, 30, 60 and 90 degrees each side of the centre reference mark.

The other main flight instrument was the Heading Indicator (Mk.5 FT compass). This combined the functions of a directional gyro and a magnetic compass and consisted basically of the azimuth gyro component of the MRG, a detector unit (in the starboard wing) which sensed azimuth orientation with respect to the earth's magnetic field, a servo-motor and monitoring signal amplifiers, and a heading indicator. The instrument could be used as a compass or as a directional gyro by pressing the COMP/DG button at the base of the unit. The SYN button rapidly synchronized the gyro and detector, and the desired heading could be set on the indicator by pushing and turning the HDG button at the bottom left of the instrument. Once set to any point on the compass card, the selected heading pointer and its reciprocal rotated with the card. Heading data were transmitted to the autopilot so that when the latter was in ILS mode, movement of the selected heading pointer resulted in aileron control being applied in the appropriate sense.

Should the MRG or the attitude indicator fail, a standby Mk.6A Artificial Horizon was included to the top left of the main panel. This was electrically operated and included a fast-erection switch that could be operated during unaccelerated flight to restore attitude information if the instrument had toppled. An indicator flag (black diagonal line on orange background) warned of power or gyro failure. An electrically driven Mk.22A sensitive altimeter capable of recording altitudes up to 100,000 ft was fitted centre-left of the main panel, and this was backed up by a pressure-operated standby altimeter (Mk.24). Other instruments included a Mk.3B Machmeter which read from 0.8 to 1.8 M, a Mk.15B Airspeed Indicator (80–750 kts), and a Mk.3P Vertical Speed Indicator (VSI) which could measure rates of climb or descent up to 4,000 ft/min. A Mk.3 accelerometer was fitted to the port coaming panel and a Mk.21 altimeter on the starboard console indicated the pressure altitude of the cockpit.

RADIO AND BLIND-FLYING AIDS

Lightning F.1 aircraft were fitted with a VHF radio installation comprising one TR.1985 and one TR.1986, the frequency range being 100–125 Mc/s and 124.5–156 Mc/s respectively. A SET1/SET2 changeover switch and two 10-channel selector switches were fitted on the radio panel on the side of the port console. Two press-to-transmit switches were fitted, one on the No. 2 throttle and one on the control column. F.1A aircraft featured a UHF radio installation, all controls being mounted on two panels that together formed a centre console under the main instrument panel.

For precision approaches a standard ARI 18011 ILS installation was installed in the aircraft. The control unit was located on the side of the port console with the indicator and marker light on the lower right of the main panel. The Lightning F.1/F.1A was also fitted with a TACAN installation (ARI 18059) that presented beacon range and heading data on one instrument. The TACAN indicator was mounted centre-bottom of the main panel to the left of the ILS.

OPERATIONAL EQUIPMENT

Two installations made up the radar fire control system – the Airborne Interception radar (AI.23) and the Pilot's Attack Sight (PAS. Mk.1). The AI.23 radar could search for and detect any aircraft in the sector of sky ahead, information being shown on the pilot's cathode ray tube display situated upper-right of the main panel. Once a target echo was recognized the radar could be locked onto the target in range, azimuth and elevation, and the target could then be tracked automatically. With radar lock-on established, an approach course to a suitable position to commence an attack was calculated by the computer. This information was then presented on the PAS. Mk.1 display unit.

The PAS. Mk.1 was a gyro sight for use in pursuit attacks using guns, rocket battery or guided weapons. Approach information (from the computer in AI.23) was shown on the display unit, which, as the approach developed into an attack, assumed the role of a predictor sight. Approach and attack information was displayed on the sight as a bright pattern collimated to infinity consisting of an aiming mark (winged circle), a range meter along the top of the display in the scale 1–12 nautical miles at two-mile divisions, a closing speed scale from-100 to +500 knots and firing bracket indicators operating in pairs to the left and right of the winged circle. During a guns attack the left pair of indicators signified a range of 3,600 ft, and the right pair the desirable firing point (computed as a function of closing speed). When using guided weapons the appearance of the indicators informed the pilot that the weapons had acquired, and that the aircraft was within firing range.

Other information consisted of a target indicator controlled by the AI.23 approach computer, which indicated a computed position corrected for an optimum approach, and a horizon bar that moved with the target indicator and showed roll rate of the aircraft. Additionally, if radar lock-on was lost, a circle of six diamonds augmented the aiming mark instead of the closing speed scale. PAS. Mk.1 controls included the master armament selector switch on the side of the starboard console. This had four positions: OFF, GUNS, GW and RB. A twist grip on the throttle lever selected either radar of manual-ranging modes. Normally left in the 'radar' position, the grip had to be lifted and turned anti-

clockwise to select 'manual'. A span-set control on the starboard side of
the PAS display unit was used for setting the estimated wingspan of a
visual target when using manual ranging, and a dimmer switch
adjusted brightness of the displays.

The AI.23 display unit had a visor fitted to minimize the effects of
bright sunlight and also had a polarized light screen interposed between
the tube and the visor, the brightness of which could be adjusted. The
vertical sides of the screen were flanked by range scales, one reading 0–7
and the other 0–28 nautical miles; azimuth position within 50 degrees
port and starboard was indicated against a horizontal scale at the
bottom of the screen. A knob on the display unit enabled the pilot to
switch the approach computer on prior to radar lock-on and to select
(for use in the computer) one of three attacker/target speed ratios
provided by ground control. Other AI.23 controls and switches were
mounted on a hand controller on the port console. This multi-function
unit was used to adjust various aspects of radar performance, including
scanner elevation and azimuth, gain control, scan pattern, range
marker, display range scale, phase change (search, acquisition and
track), AI/auto-ranging and anti-countermeasures.

The firing trigger was located on the control column. With guided
weapons selected and with missiles armed, pressure on the trigger (a
minimum of two seconds) initiated a sequence of events during which
a turbo-alternator in the missile was switched on and the weapon pack
power supply was disconnected. The homing head then locked onto the
target, the propulsion motor ignited and the missile was fired. Relevant
switches on the starboard console for a missile attack were the GW
Pairs/Single switch; the GW armed switch that controlled the guided
weapons pack alternator and missile cooling air supplies; and the GW
arming indicator, a blue light that was normally extinguished after the
two-minute arming cycle. The GW armed time indicator on the starboard coaming panel consisted of a green light that would begin to flash
when the missile cooling air and refrigerant supplies were exhausted
after approximately 15 minutes.

SIDE CONSOLES

The No. 1 and No. 2 engine throttles were mounted on the port console
just ahead of the AI hand controller. Forward of the throttles was the
undercarriage selector switch and directly above this was the brake
parachute stream handle, the jettison button being positioned to the left
of the standby artificial horizon. Just inboard of the jettison button was
the flap selector switch with a flap position indicator adjacent to the
pilot's left knee. This was also the location for the ventral tank/guided

weapon jettison handle. As F.1A aircraft were capable of flight re-fuelling, additional switches and indicator lights were fitted to a panel just to the rear of the AI hand controller. These comprised a three-position control switch and five green TANKS FULL lamps. When selecting FLIGHT REFUEL on the control switch, all tank refuelling valves opened until their respective tanks were full, whereupon the valve closed and the appropriate lamp illuminated on the indicator panel. At all other times the control switch had to be in the OFF position, otherwise fuel transfer from the ventral and flap tanks was prevented.

On the other side of the cockpit at the rear of the starboard console the cockpit altimeter and wheel brake pressure gauge were located, together with the cockpit air temperature selector. Forward of these was the autopilot controller and to the right the engine start switches. Ahead of these were the ignition switches and a range of other switch positions, including the engine master start, windscreen heaters and de-icing switches. To the right of this bank was the main warning panel, which informed the pilot of any malfunction as regards fuel and oil pressures, AC supply, turbine stall, hydraulic pressure or top temperature controls. Switches and indicators at the head of the starboard console included the IFF master switch, the jet pipe nozzle position indicator, various internal lighting switches and the guided weapon arming and selector switches.

Boscombe Down still had reservations about the layout of the cockpit of the Lightning F.1, in particular the degree of internal lighting, the fact that the vertical speed indicator was difficult to see behind the control column and the cramped scale of the Machmeter in the vital region around Mach 0.90. The task of fitting all the switches, dials and radar displays of an all-weather fighter into a single, rather cramped, cockpit had certainly not been an easy one. In the event, English Electric did a workmanlike job with the Lightning, but the aircraft's complexity put the onus on the pilot as never before to learn the layout of the cockpit. In this respect at least, the introduction of flight simulators proved to be invaluable.

CHAPTER SEVEN

Lightning versus U-2

Although the Lightning could out-perform all other contemporary jet fighters in the climb and was capable of operating at heights in excess of 60,000 ft, such high levels of performance led to something of a dilemma. Very few aircraft were capable of operating at such heights, and even by late 1962 (by which time the Lightning had been in squadron service for over two years) it had still not been possible to investigate realistically the ultra-high-level interception capability of the Lightning, as high-flying targets were just not available. This situation was to change, however, in October 1962 when the USAF based a detachment of Lockheed U-2 reconnaissance aircraft at Upper Heyford. This deployment had been planned for some time and was part of the High Altitude Sampling Program (HASP), which was set up to capture fall-out particles from Soviet nuclear tests. Seizing this unexpected opportunity, the RAF requested, and received, permission to carry out practice interceptions as the U-2s went about their daily business.

A trial was conducted by AFDS using two Lightning F.1As made available by RAF Wattisham. As the U-2s were being flown on a northerly track over the Pennines and central Scotland, the Lightnings were based at Middleton St George, and special clearance was given for supersonic flight over land, as long as this did not occur within 25 miles of a major built-up area. The rules of engagement were strict: interceptions were limited to visual ident passes, and if visual contact had not been made by 5 nm range, the 'attack' had to be broken off. The Lightnings were also not to approach closer than 5,000 ft astern of the target and on no account were they to pass in front. Throughout the trial each Lightning carried a ventral tank and two Firestreak acquisition rounds, specialist advice being provided by English Electric on the best theoretical profiles for each type of interception.

The trial was divided into three phases, involving interceptions at 60,000 ft, 65,000 ft, and heights in excess of 65,000 ft. Before each phase, practice flights were made without a target, usually over the North Sea. The U-2s were initially intercepted on their outbound flights, but as techniques were perfected they were also engaged on their return. To obtain maximum experience from a limited number of runs, two Lightnings usually flew as a pair, control being the responsibility of Buchan radar, with Patrington acting as a secondary station for early warning, scramble and recovery. Pilots taking part wore a Mk.5 anti-g suit, a Taylor-Baxter pressure helmet and a long-sleeved partial-pressure jerkin, the latter being made available especially for the trial.

As the interceptions were being carried out above the Lightning's thrust boundary, a technique had to be evolved using the principle of the energy climb, whereby speed was traded for height. Various profiles were planned, the object being to place the fighter at the inter-cept height with sufficient speed to enable it to close with the target before minimum control speed was reached. One of the biggest prob-lems at high altitude is that Indicated Air Speed (IAS) decreases as height is gained to a point where it eventually coincides with stall speed, which remains constant. At 60,000 ft the Lightning's minimum practical control speed was about 190 kts IAS, but this corresponded to a Mach number of around 1.0, leaving only a small margin between arrival and break-off speeds. Another factor was the relatively slow speed of the U-2, which cruised at around 135 kts IAS/0.7 M at 60,000 ft. But despite all the difficulties, a number of successful interceptions were carried out.

The initial intercepts were carried out at 60,000 ft, a total of eleven sorties being flown to evolve a satisfactory flight profile, with a further seven sorties leading to actual interceptions. The technique eventually adopted was to carry out a cold power climb to 36,000 ft, at which height a turn was made onto the crossing vector and a maximum reheat acceleration started up to 1.5 M. When this speed had been achieved a constant Mach climb to 50,000 ft was set up, followed by a turn onto the target's heading. On receipt of the controller's instruction a 10-degree snap-up was initiated, and this angle of climb was held until 60,000 ft was reached at a speed of approximately 1.2 M. It was found that this height could be held for about 1 minute 20 seconds, by which time IAS had reduced to such a degree that positive control became difficult.

The technique adopted for interceptions at 65,000 ft differed markedly. Because of the extra height, acceleration was extended so as to reach 1.7 M, and once this had been achieved a constant Mach climb to 50,000 ft was initiated. The best angle of climb for the final zoom proved to be problematical. A 10-degree climb was found to be too shallow and the ground distances were so great that they caused acute problems for the ground controllers. The ideal snap-up angle turned out to be 20 degrees, and when this was employed it enabled the Lightning to arrive at 65,000 ft with a speed of approximately 1.25 M, allowing just 30 seconds of useful time before minimum control speed was reached. Despite the extremely limited amount of time available, this profile was later proved by two successful runs against a U-2 at 65,000 ft.

During the trial eight profiles were flown to investigate the possibility of intercepting targets above 65,000 ft. The best result was obtained with an acceleration to 1.7 M at 36,000 ft, and then a constant Mach climb to 45,000 ft followed by a 25-degree zoom climb. Using this method a height of 68,700 ft was reached. It was felt that this figure was unlikely to be exceeded with the Lightning's limiting Mach number at that time (1.7 M). The profiles flown during this phase were purely experimental and no interceptions were attempted (see Figure 2 for a diagram of the recommended operational profile for the interception of a subsonic target flying at 60,000 ft).

The techniques used during these interceptions involved very accurate flying, particularly during the constant-Mach climb and the entry and completion of the zoom climb. Any harsh control movements adversely affected performance to the extent that the quoted heights were likely to be unattainable. During the constant-Mach climb from 36,000 ft the required Mach number had to be maintained, whatever manoeuvring was requested for control purposes. As for the snap-up, the entry had to be performed very gently, the aim being to set up the required angle of climb with the minimum loss of speed. During the zoom climb a very careful watch had to be made of the Machmeter and altimeter, and it was best to gradually relax the back pressure on the control column within about 5,000 ft of the intercept height. To maintain height above 60,000 ft the control column had to be kept well aft of the central position and all control movements had to be performed gently, otherwise the aircraft was likely to suffer a rapid loss in airspeed and/or height.

Despite the fact that the main object of the trials was to establish accurate flight profiles for visual ident passes, some time was available for AI handling, and the results obtained were very encouraging. Initial pick-up occurred at 15–18 miles, and the run culminated with missile acquisition at 2–3 miles, at the same altitude as the target. During the trial there were no cases of engine or reheat flame-out, although there were several instances of engine negative creep when, with full reheat selected, rpm would drop momentarily to around 94 per cent before rapidly surging to 101–102 per cent.

Towards the end of the U-2 interceptions, several Wattisham-based pilots took part in the trial, including Flt Lt Henryk Ploszek of 56 Squadron:

I was involved in Exercise Trumpet and flew a couple of sorties in a Lightning F.1A against U-2s, operating from Middleton St George. As a squadron pilot from the Wattisham Wing (together with Flt Lts Pete Ginger and Martin Bridge from 111 Sqn) we were only issued with regular pressure jerkins and so only flew the 'lower' high altitude intercepts, leaving the higher stuff to the sleeved pressure jerkin-suited CFE pilots. The sky was dark blue up there, and control was minimal at the slow indicated airspeeds, requiring gentle handling to avoid disturbing the engine intake airflow, particularly in the turn away after intercept, which had to be completed astern and well clear of the U-2, to avoid our shock waves stalling the airflow over their wings. If the flow became turbulent, the engines could surge, leading to a flame out, requiring a smart dive to lower altitude for relight.

Although the trial was successful, it did manage to cause a certain amount of controversy, as a sonic boom was planted on the city of Edinburgh on 24 October. This unfortunate occurrence came about through a number of factors, not least being the fact that the U-2 was flying 15 miles east of its normal track. At first the Air Ministry kept quiet, and various theories were explored in the local press as to what had caused the noise. The missile research establishment at Spadeadam was quickly discounted and the finger of suspicion was then aimed in the direction of a local Army bomb disposal unit. However the Army denied all allegations, the cornerstone of their case being that as the bang had been recorded at 8.41 a.m., it could not have been caused by their people because they would not have been up at such an hour! The RAF eventually had to come clean and admit that one of its aircraft had exceeded the speed of sound. (This incident also featured in newspaper cartoons, one showing a rather irate Edinburgh city gent complaining, 'A detonation, report, explosion perhaps – but not a BANG. Bangs are for Glasgow!')

From the trials carried out by CFE it was clear that the maximum effective altitude of the Lightning F.1/F.1A in the U.K. was around the 65,000 ft mark, the precise figure depending on individual aircraft performance and weather conditions, in particular the height of the tropopause and upper air temperatures. With more power and a higher limiting Mach number, the Lightning F.3/F.6 was capable of exceeding

70,000 ft. One of the highest flights ever recorded in a Lightning, however, occurred over Saudi Arabia in 1979. The pilot on this occasion was Wg Cdr Brian Carroll, who at the time was Chief Flying Instructor with the Royal Saudi Air Force:

7 August 1979 dawned fine and clear, but then I was operating out of an air base in Saudi Arabia, so these conditions were the norm, unlike flying in the UK, where poor visibility, extensive cloud and precipitation had significant effects on many flights. One of our Lightning F.53s needed a flight test, nothing too demanding, more of a jolly than anything else. Following a normal cold power climb to 36,000 ft I headed south towards the 'Empty Quarter', planning to carry out a high-speed run and then return to base.

The tropopause was pretty high on that particular day and the aircraft performed extremely well, rapidly achieving a high Mach number. About now the thought entered my head as to what altitude I could achieve, so with nothing else to do I set about finding out. By then I was about 140 nm south of base, having just completed a turn for home and still moving at around Mach 1.6 at 45,000 ft. Easing both throttles to full reheat, I lowered the nose gently and soon achieved Mach 2.1; a climb was then commenced, the speed holding remarkably well and the altimeter winding up in a most impressive way. I soon passed 70,000 ft, the aircraft showing no inclination to stop climbing. By now the sky was getting quite dark, a purplish colour, and earth curvature was beginning to be more and more apparent.

Speed was still close to Mach 2.0 and both engines were running smoothly with no sign of surge, something that can occur when the air starts to get thin, so any movement of the throttles needed to be very gentle. 85,000 ft was now showing and yet the aircraft was still easing upwards. Mach number was still high but, more significantly, the IAS was approaching the minimum below which the aircraft would stall. Very slowly the climb rate fell away and finally stopped with the altimeter reading 87,300 ft.

I had now cancelled both reheats (both engines were still running smoothly) and very gently the nose was lowered. As I carefully reduced power and started back down the slope, IAS started to increase, Mach number staying close to Mach 2.0. The situation was hardly normal in that I was close to the limiting Mach number and at the same time also close to the indicated air speed at which the aircraft would stall, so going down hill was not necessarily as simple as one might assume. A call to Air Traffic requesting a recovery was acknowledged, clearing me to 36,000 ft

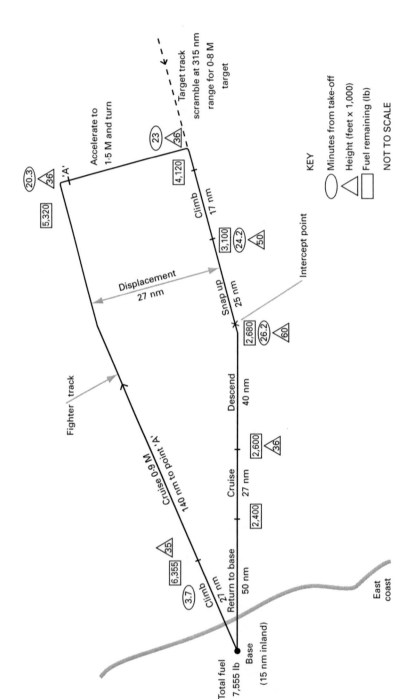

Fig. 2 Flight Profile – Subsonic Target – 60,000ft

along with the question, 'Say your height'. My response was, 'Descending through FL 700'. There was rather a long pause, followed by the same question, to which I responded, 'Descending through FL 600'. Recovery continued normally for a visual rejoin, once around the circuit and a normal touchdown.

I related this flight to a few of the other pilots at the time and made an entry in my logbook to that effect. At such an extreme altitude the aircraft was on a knife-edge; either or indeed both engines could easily have surged and possibly flamed out and that would have been, shall we say, 'bad news'. A loss of cabin pressure could have proved fatal. Additionally there was always the possibility of losing aerodynamic control. In such circumstances the aircraft could have tumbled, with every chance of a total airframe break-up (the tumble should really be described as roll/yaw coupling, allowing the aircraft to diverge from its true flight path – the result could have been wing drop, and with virtually no aerodynamic control it would most likely have fallen out of control and broken up). Extremely delicate handling was a priority to ensure that this did not occur.

You may well ask then, why did I risk this by going so high? A difficult question to answer, but if I must do so, then I would simply say, 'Why not?' Rather like people who try to break records doing free dives to extreme depths, or climbing ridiculously difficult mountains. Not that my 'high flight' could be compared with such achievements, after all I only had to sit there, enjoy the ride, wonder at the incredible view, and let the aircraft do the hard work. U-2 pilots fly higher on routine sorties, but for the Lightning it was something of a record and says everything about this great aircraft and the Rolls-Royce engines that powered it.

Brian Carroll was not the only pilot to attempt an altitude record in the Lightning. Flt Lt Dave Roome of 74 Squadron was determined to have a go in an F.6 while the Tigers were based at Tengah in Singapore in the late 1960s:

On 23 October 1968 I had the chance to intercept a USAF RB-57F, a highly modified version of the Canberra with a 122 ft wing span and 42,000 lb of thrust. This was in the Far East carrying out high altitude meteorological trials on turbulence prior to Concorde starting commercial services to Singapore. The abilities of this aircraft in the upper atmosphere were demonstrated graphically when its pilot climbed 15,000 ft, from 65,000 ft to 80,000 ft, while flying a 180-degree turn! He was surprised that the Lightning which carried out the next intercept overtook him in a descent through his altitude and he advised us that his last run would take some time to set up. This time his altitude was into six figures and he was safe, but it left me with the thought that out in the tropics, where the tropopause is in the order of 55,000 ft, the Lightning could probably achieve above 85,000 ft. I was determined to try it when I got the chance, and some months later that chance arrived.

There was a Victor tanker returning from Hong Kong and offering about 17,000 lb of fuel to us. I went up the east coast of Malaysia almost to the Thai border and filled to full. I was now left with a straight run home and the east coast was the area in which we could fly supersonic. Initially I climbed to 50,000 ft, which was the subsonic service ceiling of the aircraft, and there I accelerated to 2.0 M and started a zoom climb, selecting about 16 degrees of pitch. I levelled off at 65,000 ft and let the aircraft have its head, reaching 2.2 M before once again flying the same zoom profile. This time I held the climb attitude, though to do so required an increasing amount of aft stick as the reduction in downwash over the tail increased. Eventually the stick reached the back stops and I gently topped out, 200 ft short of 88,000 ft. From there, Singapore looked tiny and I convinced myself that I could see from the very southern tip of Vietnam over my left shoulder, past the Borneo coast in my 11 o'clock, to the western coast of Sumatra on my right-hand side. The sky was pitch black above me and all of a sudden I realized that I did not belong here. With idle/idle set, I started a glide back down which would have carried me over 150 miles. A marvellous example of the Lightning's sheer performance, though the pressure jerkin, g-suit and normal oxygen mask would not have been sufficient had the pressurization failed.

Throughout this chapter a number of references have been made to the tropopause. In the following brief summary, Brian Carroll explains its significance:

Although the composition of the atmosphere remains unchanged up to great heights, certain conditions do change. Lower layers are identified in the first instance by the rate of change of temperature with height, the rate of fall continues regularly to a height of several kilometres which depends mainly on latitude – this layer is called the troposphere, its upper boundary is the tropopause. The height of the tropopause varies as stated with latitude, seasons and general weather conditions. Normally it is lower in arctic regions in winter and highest in tropical and equatorial regions. Since air is compressible, the troposphere contains much the greater part, around three-quarters, of the whole mass of the atmosphere. The fact that the tropopause was high on the day I managed to achieve such an altitude was assisted by these conditions, thicker air was available to a higher level than usual, so the engines were able to function better than one would normally expect.

CHAPTER EIGHT

First Impressions

For most pilots, even those with a few years experience, the Lightning was approached with a certain amount of trepidation as they were faced with the prospect of making the jump from transonic speeds to Mach 2.0+ in one go. Any initial misgivings, however, were soon shown to be unfounded, and word quickly got around that the Lightning was no more difficult to fly than the Hunter. Having flown the latter with 67 Squadron, Flt Lt (later Wg Cdr) Anthony 'Bugs' Bendell first flew the Lightning during a temporary posting to AFDS prior to becoming a Flight Commander with 111 Squadron. The following comes from his autobiography, *Never In Anger* (Orion, 1998):

> My Lightning conversion on the AFDS was a one-off case. First I had to attend the Aeromedical Training Centre at RAF Upwood to be fitted with the necessary high-altitude partial-pressure clothing; the Lightning could easily exceed 60,000 ft, which fully justified specialist equipment. Much research had been done on the medical aspects of flight at high altitude. As a general rule, the cockpits of modern military aircraft were pressurized to a nominal maximum of 25,000 ft, but the pilot also needed protection in case of pressurization failure. The simple pressure-demand oxygen system fitted to the Hunter gave protection up to 45,000 ft. Above this altitude, even breathing pure oxygen, the partial pressure available to the lungs was insufficient to sustain consciousness – even for an emergency descent. For adequate protection, oxygen had to be delivered at increased pressure. This pressure breathing effectively reversed the normal pattern of respiration – oxygen was forced into the lungs and a conscious effort was needed to exhale.
>
> In the Lightning, external support for the pilot's body was provided by a combination of the g-suit and a partial-pressure jerkin. The g-suit was similar to that used in the Hunter, but in the

Lightning it also served as the lower half of a partial-pressure garment, while an inflatable jerkin, which balanced the increased oxygen pressure, gave protection to the chest and trunk. The wearing of an air ventilated suit to combat heat stress was optional. I was fitted with the latest type of protective helmet and a 'P'-type oxygen mask. On the Lightning, to simplify strapping-in procedures, all connections between the pilot and the aircraft were achieved through a single personal equipment connector which mated with the ejector seat. Finally I was measured for a Taylor helmet – a close-fitting helmet and collar – to protect my head and neck, enabling pressure breathing above 56,000 ft. Now I could begin practical training.

I remember being strapped like a helpless blue beetle in an ejection seat rig, with sensors attached to wrists and ankles, recording my pulse and blood pressure while breathing against ever-increasing oxygen pressures. A positive pressure of 20 millimetres of mercury caused minimum problems, but as the pressure increased, so did the discomfort. At 80 millimetres (equivalent to 1.5 lb p.s.i.) – the maximum pressure bearable without the Taylor helmet – my eyes felt as though they were about to pop out of their sockets and the veins on the back of my hands stood out like knotted purple cords.

One of the known side effects of pressure breathing is to develop a raging thirst – which was no problem for any self-respecting fighter pilot, but for three days, the combination of pressure breathing and drinking to slake one's thirst was an exhausting process. Then it was into the chamber for an explosive decompression – from a simulated 22,000 ft to 56,000 ft in three seconds. The equipment performed well but it was a relief when the chamber run was over.

At Coltishall I spent eleven hours in the simulator before flying my first Lightning sortie. There was no dual Lightning, so the first flight was also a first solo and thus it was very exciting. Even at idling power I had to ride the brakes to curb the acceleration. The main tyre pressures were a rock-hard 350 lb p.s.i., but the long-stroke undercarriage smoothed out the bumps. In the Lightning F.1 it was not necessary to use reheat for take-off: even in cold power, nosewheel lift-off at 150 knots occurred well within ten seconds of brake release. As one wag on 74 Squadron was later heard to comment, 'I was with it all the way, until I released the brakes on take-off!'

Once airborne, the critical speeds were not much different from the Hunter, but the acceleration was much faster and I had my work cut out to stay ahead. Care was needed not to exceed the undercarriage limit of 250 knots, but with the undercarriage retracted and with full reheat applied for a maximum-rate climb, the Lightning really lifted its skirts. The initial rate of climb was in the order of 50,000 ft per minute at an angle of 65 degrees. This would hold the speed at 450 knots until converting to Mach 0.90 at about 13,000 ft (many pilots, on their first Lightning sortie, did not transfer quickly enough to the Machmeter and found themselves surging through 18,000 ft at speeds well in excess of Mach 1.0).

The Lightning was very positive on the controls throughout the speed range. After an action-packed thirty minutes at altitude, it was time for the recovery. With the tactical air navigation equipment (TACAN) it was possible to self-navigate back to the airfield, even in bad weather, without assistance from ground control.

The Lightning was remarkably docile at low speed, although the circuit was marginally wider than I had been used to in the Hunter, and the touchdown at 165 knots was noticeably quicker. Once on the ground, the nosewheel had to be positively lowered on to the runway to make room for the brake parachute to deploy from beneath the tail. In the event of brake parachute failure, the standard procedure was to overshoot but, as I gained experience, this kneejerk reaction seemed to be questionable. In theory it was better to avoid having to make a time-critical decision, but there were occasions – for example bad weather or a critical fuel state – when launching back into the air was definitely unwise. In my opinion the decision on whether or not to overshoot was best made at the time, although I usually preferred to stay down. In fact, brake parachute failures were comparatively rare.

The Lightning F.1 was extremely short range, and a jettisonable ventral tank carrying an additional 2,000 lb of fuel was fitted as standard. Even then the total fuel capacity was only 7,500 lb. To put this into perspective, although the Lightning could cruise economically at altitude, consuming a meagre 60 lb of fuel a minute, with full reheat its consumption increased tenfold to 600 lb a minute. The actual transition to supersonic flight was hardly noticeable, but having effortlessly slipped through to Mach 1.3 the Lightning was clearly in its element. On one occasion I was asked to determine the maximum sustainable rate of turn at Mach 1.3 at 36,000 ft with full reheat selected. I found it difficult to hold the speed down to Mach 1.3 even with 80 degrees of bank applied and increasing 'g'. Obviously this sort of performance could be used to advantage in visual conditions, but it was hardly the sort of manoeuvre a pilot would wish to employ on a dark night with his head buried in the AI radar scope.

On completion of his pilot training, Plt Off Dave Jones joined 74 Squadron (Hunter F.6) in August 1958 at Horsham St Faith. Two years later he was lucky enough to be one of the first service pilots to fly the Lightning F.1 at Coltishall:

We were soon informed that we were to be the first Lightning Squadron and in June 1960 the first Lightning arrived. The boss (Sqn Ldr John Howe) was the first to fly the aircraft with the Flight Commanders and more senior pilots next. Eventually it was my turn and my first solo was on 23 September 1960 – a day I shall always remember!

The conversion on to this fine aeroplane actually started several months before with an Aviation Medical course when we were fitted out with special flying clothing – a pressure jerkin and a 'Taylor' helmet, etc. We also had the excitement of an explosive decompression from 25,000 ft to 56,000 ft in the decompression chamber at RAF Upwood to simulate losing a canopy at high altitude. This was followed by a week or so of ground school and then a dozen trips in the Flight Simulator, which, although quite good for its time, was very basic by modern standards.

The spirit and morale on 74 Squadron at this time was quite extraordinary. We were all very excited at the prospect of flying the Lightning and proud that it was 74 that had been chosen to be the first squadron. But I (and I am sure that I was not alone) certainly had a slight worry that I might not be able to cope. The Hunter was a Mach 1 aircraft – just supersonic in a dive, whereas the Lightning was a Mach 2 aircraft and very supersonic, even in a climb! However in the event it was quite easy to fly and everyone on the squadron converted onto the Lightning without any problems.

I remember on my first solo taking a deep breath before releasing the brakes and then concentrating very hard and trying to remember all I had been told . . . keep it straight . . . check 100 per cent rpm and jet pipe temperature within limits . . . get the nosewheel up by 135 kts . . . get airborne at 165 kts . . . if you go too fast on the runway you will strip the tread off the tyres . . . when safely airborne, undercarriage up . . . make sure the nosewheel is 'up and locked' before 250 kts . . . try not to go supersonic in the climb . . . watch the Mach number . . . and so on! The first trip was fairly straightforward, nothing too dramatic. Take-off – climb to 36,000 ft – accelerate to Mach 1.3 – a few turns – slow down to subsonic – descend and return to Coltishall for a GCA – overshoot and land off the next GCA. The landing speed of the Lightning was much higher than the Hunter and I remember the relief when the brake chute opened and the aircraft slowed down and was obviously going to stop before the end of the runway. I was now confident that I could cope!

In the early days of the Lightning the conversion process was carried out by a small unit that toured the operational squadrons. It was commanded by Sqn Ldr John Robertson:

> In early 1960 I was posted to RAF Coltishall as OC Lightning Conversion Unit (LCU) with the brief of converting the Hunter squadrons to the Lightning. I went to CFE at Leconfield in June 1960 and converted to the Lightning flying development-batch aircraft. Afterwards we set up the ground school and devised twelve exercises for pilot conversion, also writing the safety drills and procedures. Our aircraft were late and in August I flew one of the first F.1 aircraft from Warton to Coltishall (XM166). We converted 74 Squadron first, flying chase in a Hunter on first solos. We then went to Wattisham (commuting daily) and converted 56 Squadron in January 1961, followed by 111 Squadron.

Flt Lt Mike Shaw also flew with 74 'Tiger' Squadron and later flew F-4B Phantoms during an exchange posting with the US Marine Corps at Cherry Point, North Carolina, before becoming a member of the RAF Handling Squadron at Boscombe Down, specializing in the Lightning and Phantom. He recalls his introduction to the Lightning F.1 in 1962, by which time the LCU had become the Lightning Conversion Squadron (LCS) and had its own base at Middleton St George (now Teesside Airport):

> As I neared RAF Coltishall to join my new squadron I became aware of concentrated jet noise. Still some three miles away, I stopped the car and got out to see a Lightning flying quite slowly, almost inverted, at about 3,000 ft. Arriving at the Officers' Mess I was in time to see five Lightnings in a wide 'vic' fly over the airfield at high subsonic speed. It was impressive, and noisy! After checking in, I drove back to a point on the quiet country road at the threshold of the duty (north-easterly) runway to watch the five aircraft land. Each swept by at surprisingly high power settings,

noticeably faster than the familiar Hunter, but with their ponderous, gleaming slab-sided fuselages at an alarmingly high angle of attack. The tail-ends didn't (quite) touch the runway and all five drag chutes did their stuff.

I had witnessed 'A' Flight practising for SBAC Farnborough, which was to be held about three months later in September 1962. What I had missed, though, was the reheat rotation take-off – I'd just heard it. The aircraft would take the runway, then release the brakes at 3-second intervals. The engines would then be brought up from 80 to 100 per cent rpm, when reheat would be selected. When both had stabilized, the airspeed would be whistling through 100 kts, and at 125 kts the nosewheel would be lifted off. The gentle rotation would be continued to achieve take-off attitude at 175 kts. Once airborne, the undercarriage was retracted. The main legs went back and outwards, twisting flat as they went (very clever hinges), but the nosewheel retracted forwards and sometimes didn't make it! At 220 kts (for the F.1 and T.4) the stick could be pulled fully back to kill 30 kts, then centred to hold 190 kts. Lift was then provided by the engines, giving about 70 degrees angle of climb. As the ejection seat rails were inclined 23 degrees back from the vertical, the pilot's back was roughly horizontal. Exhilarating? Spectacular? Yes. Dangerous? Only if an engine failed or the pilot let adverse yaw develop, something that Tigers never did in those days!

Not long after my arrival at Coltishall the LCS began forming at Middleton St George with Lightning T.4s, and so after a few weeks of flying 74 Squadron's two Hunter T.7s, I became one of the first four students to go there. The CO was Wg Cdr Ken Goodwin, a superb ex-Hunter aerobatic display pilot renowned for negative-g manoeuvres! The instructors I flew with during my week's stay were Flt Lts Geoff Steggall, Roly Jackson and Donald Donaldson-Davidson, a navigator and specialist on the AI.23 radar and known as 'D-D'. The LCS gave me nine sorties in five days, demonstrating a very impressive serviceability rate. This was not, of course, the full conversion course, but it was a valuable introduction to the aircraft, and the four students (Wg Cdr Luke, Flt Lts Chris Bruce, 'Bodger' Edwards and myself) were probably useful fodder for the instructors to get their teeth into!

Although the Lightning had conventional aerodynamic flight controls, the low-set slab tailplane gave the pilot pitch control even when the airflow over the mainplane was hopelessly disturbed, so the aircraft could be 'blown' round corners by increasing the angle of attack of the fuselage (and therefore the engines) and using the power. It was vectored thrust, when the wings had all but given up providing lift! In those circumstances, the wings were simply somewhere to put the fuel, wheels and ailerons. The landing was demanding. With an approach (GCA or ILS) speed of 175 kts and an over-the-hedge last-look speed of 165 kts, a good drag chute was essential as the wheel brakes could not absorb the energy. Indeed if brake pressure were still applied when the taxiing speed dropped to about 20 kts or so, the brakes could weld solid. A chuteless landing without a stiff headwind was always a delicate affair, often ending in the Mk.12 Safeland Barrier!

The Lightning felt, and was, immensely strong and beautifully built. It handled positively and was comfortably stable about all three axes. It was reluctant to spin and (I'm told) would recover immediately when back pressure on the stick was reduced. The designers and test pilots had done their jobs. Squadron pilots were confident ('cocky', some others might say) in the knowledge that nothing in Europe in the early 1960s could get near to or out-fly them; they felt superior because, strapped to a Lightning, they were superior!

Flt Lt Peter Vangucci, also of 74 Squadron, first encountered the Lightning when he attended No. 6 Course at LCS:

I finally reached Middleton St George in May 1963 after a Meteor refresher course following a four-year ground tour, having been with 74 (F) Squadron at Coltishall on and off since the previous December. I soloed on 30 May in T.4 XM972 following five trips with my instructor, Flt Lt Kit Thorman. During my dual conversion I can remember Kit saying, 'If you go inadvertently into reheat [rather easy to do as the reheat detent was not very positive] on your first solo it's safer not to bother cancelling until airborne.' Naturally I went into reheat and, against all instructions, just as quickly cancelled it as I was having enough trouble keeping up with the aircraft in cold power, let alone reheat! Thereafter the flight was uneventful although the weather was pretty awful, indeed just about every sortie throughout the conversion course involved instrument flying and/or an instrument approach.

As well as the training of pilots for the operational squadrons, many high-ranking officers also took the Lightning conversion course, including Gp Capt (later AVM) 'Paddy' Harbison, who had flown Spitfires with 118 Squadron during the Second World War and F-86 Sabres with the USAF's 335th Tactical Fighter Squadron in the Korean War. He first flew the Lightning in December 1963 prior to taking command of RAF Leuchars:

My checkout on the Lightning came via my instructor Flt Lt Bernie Ibison and was quite straightforward. The ground instruction was comprehensive, aircraft systems, electrics, etc. were well covered as were the emergencies which seemed to be numerous. The simulator instruction was tremendously valuable although not initially very popular with pilots new to the idea. It was a great training aid leading progressively to the final session where every possible emergency was inflicted on the unfortunate student in one sortie. It did little for his confidence or peace of mind, but served the purpose.

The dual-control T.4 cockpit was tight with both pilots sitting off the central line, which took a little adjustment. My reflections on the checkout and first flight were of concern mainly over fuel endurance. Start-up and take-off had been well covered in the simulator, but the first real take-off was exhilarating, especially the very noticeable acceleration when the afterburners were selected and the staggering rate of climb. Altitude was reached very quickly but even so the fuel gauges had moved a disturbing amount. The Lightning handled superbly and time passed quickly.

The approach and landing differed from previous fighters in that the glide path was much flatter, very much so, and power was maintained all the way to the runway where the flare was minimal. In the event that the drag chute did not deploy, a go-around was recommended and a low precautionary approach made for the next landing as the brakes were not over-effective and tended to overheat and fade. First solo was made in the T.4 and in my case the next flight was in an F.1. The supersonic demo flight was a non-event in the Lightning other than the speed at which fuel was consumed. It would be true to say that the Lightning was one of the hard-landing breed of aircraft, very similar to the F-100, and its very thin high-pressure tyres had little give. On my second trip the weather deteriorated to Yellow 3 which required GCA assistance which I thought was stretching things somewhat in the event of a diversion.

The Lightning pilot workload was extremely high, and it was some time before first-tour pilots were posted to Lightning squadrons. First-class flying training and close supervision enabled this step to be taken. Although the Lightning was under-armed it was well suited for its role as an interceptor under close GCI control. Compared to contemporary fighters of the day it was in the Ferrari class and was much loved by those who flew it.

CHAPTER NINE

Lightning F.3 Service Release and Tactical Trials

T he Lightning F.1 was followed into service by the F.2, which was externally similar to the F.1A (except for an intake duct on the spine for the DC stand-by generator) but had partial OR946 flight instrumentation, an offset TACAN and a liquid-oxygen breathing system. It also featured a fully variable reheat system. The F.2 was quickly followed by the F.3, XG310 of the Development Batch being modified to become the F.3 prototype. By the end of the year sufficient aircraft were available for a handling and performance assessment to be carried out by A&AEE at Boscombe Down.

In comparison with the Lightning F.2, the principal changes with the F.3 were as follows:

1) Increase in maximum permissible weight for take-off and all forms of flying (including landing) from 34,500 lb to 35,500 lb.

2) Increase in fin area by 11½ per cent.

3) 'Fueldraulic' fuel system with wing-to-wing transfer and a gauging system for the 250 gal ventral tank.

4) Avon 301 engines in place of Avon 210.

5) Aileron restriction to 8 degrees (except when the undercarriage was lowered, in which case the full 16 degrees of movement was available).

6) Larger jacks for lowering the undercarriage.

7) A cross-linked hydraulic system for the flaps, which reduced the possibility of asymmetric flap operation.

8)   Deletion of gun armament and provision for carriage of Red Top missiles.

9)   Cockpit instrument and equipment changes – Air Data System Mk.2 and strip speed display in place of Air Data System Mk.1 and conventional speed display. AI.23B radar with S-Band Homer and Standby Light Fighter Sight in place of AI.23B and PAS.

The Lightning aircraft used in the trial were XG310, XN734, XP693 and XP694 (XP699 was used later for night assessment), and the flight envelope was bounded by 700 kts IAS, 2.1 IMN and 63,000 ft. Normal accelerations were limited to 6.5 g (subsonic with ventral tank feeding or empty), 6.5 g (supersonic up to 1.8 IMN with ventral tank empty), 6.0 g (supersonic up to 1.8 IMN with fuel in ventral tank), 4½ g (between 1.8 and 2.0 IMN) and 2 g (above 2.0 IMN). There was an overriding limit of 3½ g and 1.8 IMN with a single missile.

During acceleration, the yawing impulse at transonic speed was found to be less than on the F.1/F.2. The rudder position for straight and level flight with two Red Tops varied from a small amount of rudder to port at low speeds to about two degrees starboard at 2.0 IMN. When the port missile only was fitted, three degrees of starboard rudder was required at the same IMN. This represented 70 per cent of the available feel trimming range. Strangely, about the same amount of starboard rudder was required at 2.0 IMN with the starboard missile fitted. This could not be explained, but it was felt that if all aircraft were of this standard there would be little embarrassment in service.

Limiting values of normal acceleration were applied in turning flight at conditions as near the limiting design stressing points as possible and over a wide range of CG positions, the aim being to exceed the proposed service limits by margins of 0.1 IMN, 50 kts IAS and 0.5 g. At the limiting conditions of IMN and IAS, stick forces and stick force per 'g' were satisfactory and well within stick force gradient requirements. However, as the gradient was substantially constant over the full travel, the forces necessary to pull maximum 'g' were well outside the requirements, particularly for aircraft without missiles. It was felt that Red Top attacks would not be adversely affected, as higher normal accelerations were generally not used.

The most sensitive region for longitudinal control was subsonic, at about 0.9 IMN and 525 kts with two Red Tops. However, control lightness was deemed acceptable, provided pilots were sufficiently briefed of the situation. In the event of the ventral tank failing to transfer its contents, CG moved aft as the main fuel tank was used up and longitudinal stability reduced. As the ventral tank was gauged on the F.3 (unlike previous marks) any problems would be immediately apparent to the pilot, and it was considered that an experienced pilot would have no difficulty landing with an aft CG, provided that he did not engage in rapid manoeuvres at low speeds on the approach. In this condition 2 g was not to be exceeded. In terms of maximum 'g' the F.3 with two Red Top missiles had a boundary about 1 g less at 1.7 IMN when compared with an F.1 armed with two Firestreaks. The difference decreased with decrease in IMN, so that at 1.3 the boundary was the same for both. Despite this the specification was fulfilled and the available 'g' was sufficient for all types of attacks.

Particular attention was paid to the Lightning F.3's handling with regard to lateral and rolling manoeuvres, as it was well known that the F.1/F.2 was prone to inertia coupling during rapid rolls. This investigation was carried out to determine the lateral handling in all parts of the flight envelope and the level of structural loads during rapid lateral manoeuvres under the worst conditions. To ease the problem of inertia coupling, the F.3 had aileron angle restricted to 8 degrees when the undercarriage was raised, but this led to low rates of roll in some parts of the flight envelope. The limits for the trial were as follows:

1)   180-degree rapid rolls at IMN up to 1.8 and at 'g' values 1–4 g (3 g with a single missile).

2)   360-degree rapid rolls between 300 kts and 0.9 IMN at heights between sea level and 15,000 ft. Limited to 1 g entry condition and symmetrical configuration.

3)   360-degree slow rolls at IMN up to 1.8 for 1 g entry condition and symmetrical configuration.

Fin loads were measured while rolling rapidly under high positive 'g'. The technique adopted was to roll from a level turn at the required 'g' in one direction to a level turn at the same 'g' in the other direction with little or no tailplane or rudder input. The maximum fin loads measured were about 75 per cent at subsonic speeds (0.8–0.9 IMN) at 30,000 ft in conditions of moderate buffet. It was established that the combination of buffet level and aircraft attitude relative to the flight path was a reasonably good indication of the limiting incidence to maintain fin loads at about the 75 per cent level. Other conditions for high fin load were 1.3 IMN/650 kts and 1.8 IMN/650 kts, particularly when only carrying one missile.

Roll rates under high positive 'g' varied considerably and were a function of 'g' and Mach number. In the 4 g case, rate of roll at 0.9 IMN was in the order of 70 degrees per second, this figure then reducing in linear fashion to a low point of only 5 degrees per second at 1.3 IMN. Thereafter roll rates increased again with increase in Mach number so that at 1.6 IMN rate of roll was around 35 degrees per second. The minimum roll rate value at 1.3 IMN was due to the fact that at this Mach number the yawing moment caused by the use of aileron was at its maximum, together with a steady deterioration in directional stability with increased Mach. This combination meant that if aileron was applied to roll to the left, the yawing moment to the right produced by the ailerons tended to offset rolling effectiveness. The degradation in rate of roll could be reduced to some extent by using rudder to counter the aileron yaw, and by reducing normal acceleration. Care had to be taken, however, not to use rudder at the highest Mach numbers as, because of the greatly reduced directional stability, there was a strong possibility of dangerous sideslip being produced. The yawing moment when carrying a single missile could be additive to the aileron yaw and reduce roll rate still further. Conversely it could increase the rate of roll when rolling 'towards' the missile.

Further rolling tests confirmed predictions that 360-degree rolls could be performed from wings level at 1 g and using the maximum (8-degree) movement. Provided that the aircraft was symmetrical, no handling difficulties were experienced and fin loads were acceptable. It was stressed, however, that fore-and-aft control column movements and movement of the rudder should be kept to a minimum so that there was no danger of approaching conditions for autorotation, and it was recommended that aileron control only be used. Low-rate 360-degree rolls were also investigated at supersonic speeds, the entry conditions again being 1 g, wings level. Roll rates between 40 and 60 degrees per second were obtained, some rudder and elevator movement being deemed acceptable in this case as there was little danger of autorotation. Course-changing turns were carried out at maximum allowable 'g' and at 1.8–2.0 IMN without difficulty, and some manoeuvres were also investigated at less than 1 g. It was established that the probability of high fin load while pushing over and turning to attack a target below the aircraft was very low.

After a simulated missile attack on a target above the Lightning, the breakaway manoeuvre could be achieved effectively by rolling through 120 degrees in the direction in which the aircraft was already banked and by pulling about 3 g until the nose of the aircraft was 30 degrees below the horizon. If the target was below the Lightning the wings could be levelled and 3 g applied until the aircraft was 30 degrees nose up. These techniques gave a satisfactory separation between the target and the attacking aircraft. Fin loads were not measured for the worst-case condition of firing and breakaway, but simulator studies showed that the loads were likely to be somewhat greater than those during rapid rolling. This was because of the yawing impulse as the missile left the aircraft. Loads could be reduced if the pilot corrected the sideslip with rudder before rolling and by relaxing 'g' while rolling to the near inverted attitude. Use of autostabilizer was recommended as it tended to reduce the yawing impulse on firing.

On earlier marks of Lightning, flight with a refuelling probe attached had been restricted to subsonic speeds, but with the F.3 handling trials were carried out at speeds in excess of Mach 1.0. No difficulties were encountered and it was agreed that the Lightning could be cleared for flight up to 1.7 IMN/525 kts with a probe fitted.

Much attention was also given to intake and engine performance, and it was found that under certain circumstances it was possible for the engine not to accept the airflow into the intake, a condition known as intake 'buzz'. A warning of this condition was usually given to the pilot in the form of vibration produced when the boundary layer separated from the nose cone. In extreme cases a loud audible bang was followed by the aircraft shuddering. Buzz was most likely to occur when throttling back to less than 100 per cent rpm at 1.8 IMN+ and when pulling 'g' at 1.8–2.0 IMN. It was confirmed, however, that buzz conditions induced by throttling back did not seriously affect engine performance and did not cause flame-out.

Rapid throttle movements were made at altitudes from sea level to 50,000 ft. Acceleration times were satisfactory and there was no sign of stagnation. The only indication of engine instability was when decelerating through 1.1–1.2 IMN at about 58,000 ft using maximum throttle setting without reheat. At 1.2 IMN rough running and bangs from the engine caused the pilot to throttle back. On one occasion he did not and a bang surge was recorded. During the instability rpm fluctuated ±2 per cent and the traces revealed fluctuations in compressor delivery pressure and inlet guide vane angles. Relighting was demonstrated up to 40,000 ft and 0.9 IMN. For a cold engine this process (from pressing the relight button to slow idle) took from 8 seconds at 20,000 ft to 12 seconds at 40,000 ft.

The maximum altitude at which reheat could be lit with certainty varied from 38,000 ft at 0.9 IMN to 55,000 ft at 1.7 IMN. Above these altitudes the reliability of lighting fell rapidly. Reheat selection and reselections under conditions of 4.5–5.0 g were satisfactory over the range investigated (1.15–1.75 IMN and 450–700 kts). Reheat extinction occurred at 61,000 ft and 1.0 IMN with minimum reheat and at 58,000 ft and 1.3 IMN with maximum reheat.

Engine performance was also evaluated during the firing of Red Top missiles at 1.8 IMN and 0.9 IMN. On the first two tests only one missile fired, and on one of these occasions the engine disturbance was sufficient to cancel reheat. This proved to be the only engine malfunction during the trial. Examination of the traces revealed that engine disturbance on firing one missile was greater than when firing two. It was thought possible that in the one-missile case, the missile exhaust was swallowed by the engine, whereas in the two-missile case it was not. Subsequent engine trials suggested that engine behaviour might be more sensitive to exhaust ingestion at around 59,000 ft at the conditions under which surge had been experienced.

The overall conclusions of the trial were as follows:

> From the handling point of view the difference between the F.3 and F.2 are relatively small. The extra Mach number capability has revealed no special aircraft problems. The intake buzz conditions can be induced but the aerodynamic effects on the engine are small and any fatigue implications are not yet established. The maximum IMN of which the aircraft is capable is dependent on aircraft configuration and temperature and the duration at that Mach number is too short to cause severe aerodynamic heating problems.

> The presence of Red Top missiles has destabilized the aircraft slightly, such that at 0.9 IMN the stick force is less than the minimum acceptable under current requirements. The supersonic manoeuvring capability at any flight condition has been reduced relative to the F.2, but the F.3 can do all that is required of it in guided-weapons attacks or in auto-attack when this becomes available. A careful study was made of lateral control difficulties which can occur. These can be minimized by easing of applied 'g' and by use of rudder. Wherever possible, sideslip should be corrected before rolling rapidly in order to preserve the fatigue life of the fin.

> The engine trials were unsatisfactory in that although a reasonable standard of control was reached at the end of the trial, the confidence in the system was not great. It remains to be seen if production control units will hold their calibration and have sufficient authority to preserve the limiting conditions at all times [difficulties had been experienced with the Lucas Flow Control units which often led to JPT limits being exceeded]. The reheat lighting and burning boundaries should be improved and modifications should be made to assist reheat management.

The clearance recommendations for the Lightning F.3 were as follows:

Flight Envelope

Maximum IAS	650 kts
Maximum IMN	2.0
Maximum IMN	1.8 (single missile)
Maximum IMN/IAS	1.7/525 kts (FR probe)
Minimum speed 1 g flight, flaps and u/c up	180 kts
Minimum speed 1 g flight, flaps and u/c down	140 kts

Maximum Normal Accelerations

IMN not exceeding 0.9	+6.0 g
IMN 0.9–1.8 (fuel in ventral tank)	+5.5 g
IMN 0.9–1.8 (ventral tank empty)	+6.0 g
IMN above 1.8	+4.0 g
When carrying single missile or firing one missile or two	+3.0 g
Negative acceleration limit	-3.0 g
Maximum altitude (pending further engine trials)	60,000 ft
Maximum take-off weight	35,500 lb
Maximum normal landing weight	34,500 lb

Handling Limitations – Rolling Manoeuvres

1) Rolling through 180 degrees is permitted using full available aileron (8 degrees) up to 1.7 IMN within the range 1 g and the lower of 4 g (3 g when a single missile carried) and the onset of 'g' stall buffet. Rolls of more than 180 degrees and up to 360 degrees within the same speed limitation is also permitted with two missiles, or without missiles, but must be carried out smoothly using low rates of roll only, from 1 g entry with wings level.

2) Co-ordinated turns using low rates of roll only are permitted above 1.7 IMN or with normal accelerations greater than 4 g.

3) The minimum use of ailerons is to be made with accelerometer readings of less than 1 g at any speed.

4) Before rolling, and especially when carrying a single missile, care should be taken to minimize any sideslip with appropriate rudder application.

5) Rolling through 360 degrees is permitted using full available aileron (8 degrees), with two missiles or without missiles, at speeds from 300 to 550 kts IAS below 0.9 IMN and below 15,000 ft, subject to the following conditions: the roll must be executed from the normal upright attitude in 1 g flight and must be fully completed before any other manoeuvre is commenced; aileron control only should be employed; hesitation rolls are not permitted.

6) At all speeds rapid rolls must not be carried out with the FR probe fitted.

Following the evaluation of the Lightning F.3 for service release at Boscombe Down, tactical trials were then carried out by CFE. In charge of the trial was the OC AFDS, Wg Cdr J.R. Rogers; Sqn Ldrs P. Gilliatt and K.W. Hayr AFC acted as progress officers with Capt D. Zimmerman, USAF, and Flt Lt N.D. Want as project officers. The aircraft used were XP695 and XP696 to pre-production standard and XP749 and XP750 to full F.3 standard.

Although the overall conclusion was that the F.3 (Firestreak) was capable of taking out targets operating between 0.9 and 1.3 M, several shortcomings were identified. The Lightning's capability was dominated by its critically low fuel capacity, which, despite its greater performance over the F.1 and F.2, limited speed for interceptions to 1.5 M. Even so, careful control and planning was required for a successful interception to be made. The full intercept potential of the aircraft, therefore, could not be achieved, and this situation would remain until the introduction of the larger ventral tank on the F.6. There was also criticism of the lack of gun armament, which was a particular disadvantage during low level interceptions.

Difficulty was also experienced with the hand controller for the AI.23B, which prevented the radar being used to its full potential, and there were also problems during the launch phase of the missile system when faced with ECM. When operating against window (chaff) AI.23B had an effective capability in frontal attacks within a 20-degree semi-angle off the target nose, and a limited capability in rear attacks, again over a 20-degree semi-angle off the target's tail. Outside these areas it had no capability at all. When operating against window, therefore, it was recommended that Firestreak attacks be flown in search until in the rear cone of the target. Owing to the modified short-range display of AI.23B, the F.3 was capable of closing to 500 yards on a darkened target at night, but this was of little use, as the missile's minimum firing range was about 1,000 yards and, of course, the aircraft did not carry guns.

It was also felt that the longitudinal trim rate of the F.3 was inadequate and brought about an unnecessary increase in pilot workload, especially during interceptions that were carried out during accelerating flight. An increase in trim rate of the order of 100 per cent was called for, an opinion shared by the Handling Squadron and 'A' Squadron of A&AEE. During the final stages of an interception the pilot's full attention was needed to operate the radar, but because of the slow trim rate it was necessary for him to spend time keeping the aircraft level. Many attacks required 3–4 g to be applied fairly constantly to keep the target dot centred, and the best way to achieve this was to trim the aircraft into the manoeuvre, but the trim rate as tested made this extremely difficult.

Owing to the revised fuel system of the F.3 it was recommended that a more flexible approach be taken to single-engine flying in an attempt to save fuel. During low-level attacks it was thought that one engine could either be throttled back or shut down according to training or operational requirements, a technique that could also be used during low-level diversions. On one engine almost two extra miles could be flown for every 100 lb of fuel, representing an increase of almost 37 per cent in range. It was also felt that the improved fuel system allowed a lessening of the landing fuel states of 800 lb per side, figures that had been introduced for the F.1/F.2 because of problems with their AC and DC pumps. A figure of 800 lb per side at undercarriage lowering was suggested, which would free additional fuel to achieve an extra 40 miles' range.

During the trial the opportunity was taken to use the Lightning to intercept Hunters flying at 0.85–0.90 M at 40,000 ft in conventional battle formation with a frontal coverage of 4,000–6,000 yards. This was to assess the average visual pick-up range and to establish the minimum range by which a Hunter must break to counter a supersonic Lightning/Firestreak attack. The Lightning was positioned twenty miles astern, out of condensation trails, before accelerating to maintain 1.5 M and dropping down to below 30,000 ft to close on the centre of the formation. The visual pick-up range obtained by the Hunters varied considerably and was affected by prevailing conditions. If the Lightning climbed into the trail level it was seen immediately. It was also seen on occasions when selecting reheat, as this tended to produce a puff of condensation. The Hunters had the greatest difficulty in seeing the Lightning when the latter began its attack from a height difference of over 10,000 ft. Attacks were most readily spotted against a cloud background, but on occasion it was possible for the Lightning to approach in high cirrus or alto-stratus and thus be completely obscured.

As soon as the attacking Lightning was seen, an immediate break was called and each pair of Hunters then turned towards each other. The aim of the Lightning was to obtain acquisition and reach range outer before the breaking Hunters could develop an angle-off which would be excessive for Firestreak. Limiting angle-off was assumed to be 20–30 degrees. On this basis it became obvious that the Lightning could enter a Firestreak success zone unless the Hunters managed to break before range was closed to five miles. Of nineteen attacks carried out, visual pick-up at five miles or less occurred on fourteen occasions.

1. English Electric P.1A WG760 shortly after its first flight. This was one of the first photos to be cleared for publication, appearing in *Flight* magazine on 13 August 1954. *(Philip Jarrett)*

2. Classic view of the P.1A, showing to advantage its clean, simple lines. The leading-edge notch to prohibit spanwise flow of air is apparent. *(Philip Jarrett)*

3. Roland Beamont returns to base at the end of another sortie in WG760.
(Philip Jarrett)

4. Another view of WG760 in its original form, with straight-wing leading edges.
(Philip Jarrett)

5. WG760 after fitment of cambered leading edges. This modification reduced drag at high subsonic speeds, thereby increasing range and combat patrol time. Amazingly it did not reappear until near the end of the Lightning's development.   *(Philip Jarrett)*

6. P.1B XA847 seen in its initial configuration without ventral tank and with original fin.   *(Philip Jarrett)*

7. Roland Beamont pops the airbrakes as he formates on English Electric's Meteor camera plane. XA847 has by now been fitted with a 250 gal ventral tank, which provides a welcome increase in fuel capacity. *(Philip Jarrett)*

8. P.1B XA853 was used for aerodynamic and weapons development trials by English Electric and A&AEE. It is seen here carrying two dummy Firestreak air-to-air missiles. *(Philip Jarrett)*

9. XG331 of the Development Batch took part in Service Release Handling Trials at Boscombe Down in early 1960. Like most DB aircraft, it was fitted with a Stage 2 fin, and is seen here in distinctive markings for the 1959 Farnborough Air Show.
(Philip Jarrett)

10. After trials at Boscombe Down, XG325 went to de Havillands at Hatfield for missile testing, and is seen here carrying two Red Top missiles. *(Philip Jarrett)*

11. Formation of five AFDS Lightning F.1s comprising XM135 'D', XM136 'E', XM137 'F', XM138 'G', with XM165 at the rear. *(Philip Jarrett)*

12. After flying with AFDS, XM135 was used by 74 Squadron, 226 OCU and Leuchars Target Facilities Flight. It was passed to 60 MU Leconfield in June 1970, and was subsequently used for continuation training before being retired and flown to Duxford for preservation on 20 November 1974. *(Philip Jarrett)*

13. Dramatic view of Lightning F.1 XM147 of 226 OCU taking off from Coltishall.
(Philip Jarrett)

14. Lightning F.2 front fuselage assemblies under construction at the Strand Road plant in Preston. XN774 is at extreme left, followed by XN776, XN775 and XN777.
(Philip Jarrett)

DANGER

EJECTION
SEAT

DANGER DANGER

CHOP THRO CANOPY
FOR EMGCY RESCUE

15. Wg Cdr Jimmy Dell played a significant part in the testing of the Lightning as Fighter Command liaison officer at Warton, and later as deputy Chief Test Pilot at English Electric. Here he shows off the confines of the Lightning cockpit. *(Philip Jarrett)*

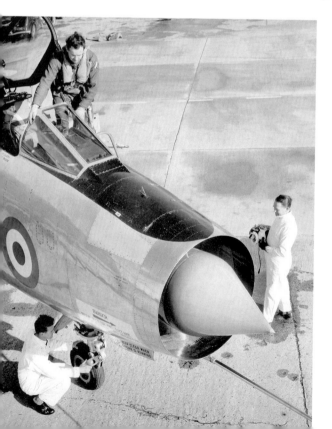

16. Posed view that serves to illustrate the height of the Lightning cockpit above ground. The neat installation of the AI.23 radar in the intake bullet is evident. *(Philip Jarrett)*

17. Lightning F.1A XM171 later flew with 56 Squadron and 226 OCU. *(Philip Jarrett)*

18. F.1A XM182 shown in early 56 Squadron markings, coded 'P'. It was later recoded 'M' and painted in the striking red and white colours of the Firebirds aerobatic team. *(Philip Jarrett)*

19. Sqn Ldr John Howe of 74 Squadron taxies out in XM143 'A', with the rest of the squadron ready to go. *(Philip Jarrett)*

20. Lightning T.4s of the Lightning Conversion Squadron near Middleton St George. The LCS was expanded to form 226 OCU and moved to Coltishall in April 1964. *(Philip Jarrett)*

21. The controversial deletion of gun armament in the Lightning F.3 meant that the aircraft's only offensive capability lay with its air-to-air missiles, either Firestreak (background) or Red Top. *(Philip Jarrett)*

22. Lightning F.3 XP695 of 11 Squadron in its element high above the clouds. *(Philip Jarrett)*

23. Close-up view of the main undercarriage of Lightning F.3 XP694 of 11 Squadron. Tyre wear could be extremely high, especially during crosswind landings, when use of the braking parachute could induce weathercocking, which in turn could lead to severe tyre scuffing. *(P.R. Caygill collection)*

24. Originally the fifth production F.3, XP697 was converted to be the first F.6 and was first flown as such on 17 April 1964 by Roland Beamont. This view shows the enlarged ventral fuel tank and twin strakes to aid directional control. *(Philip Jarrett)*

25. Lightning F.6 XR754 was one of a batch of sixteen interim aircraft which were subsequently modified to full F.6 standard, including the provision of overwing hardpoints. It is seen here on a test flight high over the Pennines. *(Philip Jarrett)*

26. Lightning F.6s of 11 Squadron in echelon port. Formation is made up of XS918 'B', XS932 'H', XS904 'A' and XS930 'F'. *(Philip Jarrett)*

27. Rapid rearming of Lightning F.6 XS923 'AA' of 5 Squadron with two Red Top missiles. *(P.R. Caygill collection)*

28. Lightning F.2 XN782 'K' of 19 Squadron was later converted to F.2A standard and flown by 92 Squadron. Its last use was as a decoy at Wildenrath before being acquired by the Flugaustellung Museum at Hermeskeil, Germany. *(Philip Jarrett)*

29. Lightning T.4 prototype XL628, which suffered fin failure during rapid rolling trials over the Irish Sea on 1 October 1959. *(via author)*

30. During a career spanning eighteen years, Lightning T.55 55-714 served with Nos 2, 6 and 13 Squadrons of the Royal Saudi Air Force before returning to the UK as ZF595 on 22 January 1986. *(Philip Jarrett)*

31. Lightning F.1s of 74 Squadron perform a typically tight wing-over in diamond nine
formation. The dangers of high-speed flight in close formation were highlighted on
16 May 1961, when XM141 lost part of its tail at low level over Coltishall.

(Philip Jarrett)

CHAPTER TEN

Lightning F.6 Handling and Performance Assessment

T he chronically short endurance of the Lightning was finally addressed with the F.6, which featured an enlarged, non-jettisonable ventral tank of 610 gallons and the ability to accommodate two overwing ferry tanks, each of 260 gallons. The revised wing planform of reduced sweep on the outer panel and increased leading-edge camber, as tested on P.1A WG760, was also adopted. Take-off weight was increased to 39,000 lb. As aileron area had been reduced slightly owing to the revised wing configuration, the travel of the ailerons was increased to ±10 degrees (±20 degrees with undercarriage down). The wheel brakes were also revised to allow for a possible increase in landing weight, and the brake parachute was strengthened so that it could be deployed at 190 kts IAS (F.3 175 kts). This was done to reduce the possibility of parachute failure and to cater for emergency high-speed landings at high weight. Prior to entering service, the F.6 was tested at Boscombe Down, most of the flying being carried out by the prototype XP697 (originally the fifth F.3 production aircraft) with production aircraft filling in where a difference existed between this machine and the production standard.

On take-off with both engines operating, performance was satisfactory for operation from 2,500 yd runways at sea level in temperatures up to ISA +30° C. Engine failures were simulated by closing the throttle of one engine to the fast idle position at 107 kts IAS and continuing the take-off. Initially the reduction in acceleration was not marked, but as speed increased the reduction became very noticeable. The aircraft left the ground at 175 kts IAS and climbed at 1,000 ft/min at 210 kts IAS with flaps and undercarriage down. After correction to ISA conditions, zero wind and runway slope, and further correcting for the thrust of the idling engine, the measured distances for a single-engine take-off were as follows:

Brakes off to 'engine throttled'	405 yd
Engine throttled to unstick	1,195 yd
Unstick to 50 feet	675 yd
TOTAL	2,275 yd

For a normal take-off the tailplane was trimmed to -7 degrees (0.3 nose down on the pilot's gauge) and the throttles opened until the brakes began to slip at about 95 per cent rpm. Reheat was then selected and successful light-up could be checked by means of the Top Temperature Control (TTC) lights in the cockpit. There was ample time to verify this and make the other engine checks before the aircraft reached 100 kts IAS. Rotation was started at 150 kts IAS using about three-quarters aft control column movement and unstick was achieved at 165–170 kts IAS. The undercarriage was retracted by the time the aircraft reached 230 kts IAS, the flaps then being retracted and reheat cancelled. Like previous marks it was found that the longitudinal trim motor was too slow in operation to achieve zero stick force for the start of the climb, and a 10–12 lb push force had to be held by the pilot.

Some take-offs were made with a more nose-down trim setting, but this led to higher and less pleasant stick forces at rotation and the 0.3 nose-down trim was preferred. The maximum crosswind encountered during take-off from a dry runway was 19 knots. As the lateral and directional handling characteristics were similar to the F.3 it was considered that the same crosswind limits could be recommended. No handling problems occurred during simulated engine failures on take-off, and a check on handling with the most forward CG position showed this to be similar to the normal case.

As XP697 did not have the uprated brakes of the production F.6, landing performance was only measured at normal weights. With fuel contents of up to 4,000 lb the approach to land was best made in the range 170–180 kts IAS, but a minimum speed of 175 kts IAS was recommended for instrument approaches irrespective of fuel state. Handling characteristics at the flare were satisfactory, and with less than 2,000 lb of fuel remaining threshold speed was around 160 kts IAS. However, if a 2-degree glidepath was flown at 170–180 kts IAS it proved to be extremely difficult to achieve the correct threshold speed because of the lower power settings, which were close to the idle/fast idle stops.

A threshold speed of 155 kts IAS was attempted from a similar approach, but this resulted in a deterioration of the aircraft's flare characteristics in that the pitch attitude achieved with normal control movements was insufficient to adequately reduce the rate of descent, and a heavy landing resulted. Under these circumstances it was easy for the pilot to misjudge the attitude of the aircraft, and over-rotation could lead to damage to the rear fuselage. Even mild turbulence on the approach could cause the strip speed indicator to give a false reading, resulting in a threshold speed 5 kts lower than intended. For this reason the recommended minimum threshold speeds were 165 kts IAS (2,000 lb fuel), 170 kts IAS (2,000–4,000 lb fuel) and 175 kts IAS for fuel states in excess of 4,000 lb.

Approaches and roller landings followed by overshoots were made at weights close to the maximum all-up weight at an approach speed of 180–185 kts IAS. No handling difficulties were encountered, although the forward view of the runway was poor because of the pitch attitude necessary during and following the flare. Flapless landings were made at speeds 10 kts IAS higher than for normal landings. In this con-figuration the view of the runway was also poor during the final stages of the landing. In addition there was a risk of hitting the runway with the tail bumper and the fins of the ventral tank. When landing at extreme aft CG, i.e. following failure of the ventral tank to transfer, stick forces were very light and control imprecise, although they remained adequate to achieve the desired approach speed.

To determine the Lightning F.6's static stability, tailplane angles to trim the aircraft in 1 g flight were measured at 2,000, 10,000 and 40,000 ft. At 2,000 ft, 650 kts IAS and without missiles, the tailplane angle required for 1 g flight was near the limit of tailplane movement in the positive sense. However, with missiles on, there was a slight improvement, and the tailplane range was sufficient for all parts of the flight envelope. Despite this, tailplane trim was still near the limit of its nose-down travel, and because full nose-up trim was never required, it was recom-mended that more nose-down trim should be made available, if necessary at the expense of the nose-up trim range.

During accelerations and decelerations at low altitude the tailplane trim rate was insufficient to maintain zero stick force. Considering the aircraft's role at the time this was thought to be acceptable, but if the Lightning was to be operated at low level at any time it was felt that a faster tailplane trim rate and more nose-down trim would be almost essential. A similar situation existed at 40,000 ft in that the F.6's nose-down trim change during acceleration was greater than the F.3 in this region, and again the tailplane trim rate was insufficient to maintain zero stick force.

At supersonic speeds the rudder was relatively ineffective over a small range about the neutral position. From the pilot's point of view this meant that if he used the rudder to maintain zero sideslip at all times, relatively large rudder angles were required, which in many cases were outside the rudder trim range. BAC recommended that this situation could be avoided if the rudder was trimmed only when the indicated sideslip exceeded half a ball width. This technique was adopted, and it was found that the directional trim range was sufficient for flight at all supersonic speeds within the flight envelope, including cases in which the aircraft carried only one missile. An additional advantage of this technique was that when the aircraft decelerated from supersonic speeds only a small amount of retrimming was needed.

The production F.6 differed slightly from the prototype. With two missiles there were no lateral, directional or longitudinal trim changes at 2,000 ft between 300 and 600 kts IAS, 0.98 IMN, while at 36,000 ft no lateral or directional trim changes were experienced up to 1.3 IMN. With a single missile it was found that by adopting the trimming technique described above no rudder trim application was necessary. On all aircraft a very slight general airframe buffet was noticed at 1.4 IMN above 30,000 ft.

Manoeuvring stability was tested in one of three ways: during constant speed or Mach number turns pulling increments of 'g' up to the maximum allowable (or the onset of buffet), decelerating turns at maximum 'g', or by rapid applications of tailplane under conditions in which the tailplane angle per 'g' was small. It was found that above 4–5 g the stick force gradient decreased significantly, but the slope remained positive up to limiting 'g' and no stick force lightening was reported by pilots. Rapid application of tailplane under these conditions indicated that it was relatively easy to achieve the proposed service limitations, especially with low fuel states, but that it was difficult to exceed these limitations by any significant margin.

Above approximately 3 g, stick force per 'g' increased considerably, and at times very high stick forces were required to obtain moderate to high 'g' increments with full tailplane. Even under these conditions it was still possible to obtain maximum 'g' values with a single-handed pull on the control column. As Mach number increased, stick force per 'g' decreased. This, coupled with a reduction in the limiting 'g' value above 1.8 IMN, made it relatively easy to exceed the limit of 4 g.

Of greater significance was a level of lateral/directional instability exhibited at high CL values around 1.2 IMN at heights above 30,000 ft, a characteristic that had first been noted by BAC. To approach the region of instability, full, or nearly full, tailplane was required, and it was char-acterized by a lack of buffet warning and a tendency to roll. Some yawing was also experienced on most occasions, release of back-pressure on the stick giving an immediate recovery. The rolling motion was preceded by a slow divergence in sideslip, but the direction of roll was not dependent on the direction of turn. The instability was not encountered above 1.35 IMN or at speeds below 1.05 IMN, where buffet cut in before any instability occurred.

Records showed that the CA Release trials of the two-seat Lightning T.5 showed similar characteristics, and the instability was also present, albeit in a less marked form, in earlier single-seat Lightnings. The most dangerous time for the instability to occur was at low supersonic Mach number in a decelerating turn, as it was possible for a spin to develop when the aircraft became subsonic and was subject to the transonic nose-up trim change; indeed, by the time of the trial one such case had already occurred. Under most circumstances restricting longitudinal manoeuvres to those using a single-handed pull force on the control column prevented the aircraft from entering the region of instability, although it was recognized that this was a most unsatisfactory way of expressing a flight limitation. Tests were also made to check damping during short-period oscillations in the speed range 0.7–2.0 IMN, the F.6 generally complying with requirements, with or without auto-stabilizers.

In common with other Lightning trials, rapid rolling was carried out, but on only one occasion was the maximum acceptable fin load exceeded. This occurred during a roll in moderate buffet at 0.9 IMN, but it was thought that a service pilot would be unlikely to get into such a situation. However, this incident did emphasize the point that limits dependent on buffet levels were not very satisfactory, and it was recom-mended that some form of incidence indicator light would give the pilot better guidance.

Rate of roll could be increased by counteracting aileron yaw with rudder and by reducing normal accelerations. This technique was recommended for conditions where the rate of roll was low, particularly around 1.3 IMN, but it was not to be used above 1.5 IMN, as directional stability was approaching its minimum and there was a strong possi-bility of dangerous sideslip being developed. As with the F.3, when rolling with a single missile and using only small rudder deflections, the rate of roll was markedly less when rolling 'away' from the missile (i.e. rolling to starboard with a port missile). At 1.3 IMN/650 kts IAS at 4 g the rate of roll was 15–20 degrees per second, which was considered just about acceptable for the breakaway manoeuvre after an attack. When rolling 'towards' the missile, rate of roll was about 30–40 degrees per second. The use of rudder prior to rolling to reduce sideslip resulted in a very heavy pedal force of approximately 200 lb at 1.3 IMN.

Handling characteristics were assessed in the event of the ventral fuel tank failing to transfer its contents to the wing tanks. Two separate systems were available for the transfer of fuel – an air pressure transfer system and an AC pump. Failure of both led to an extreme aft CG, and in this condition the F.6 exhibited positive static stability, in both the clean and landing configurations; however, there was sluggish recovery following longitudinal displacement, and the stick forces to apply 'g' were very small. Given ventral tank transfer failure, it was recommended that gentle manoeuvres only be flown (not less than +1 g and no more than +2 g) with a maximum speed of 260 kts IAS or 0.8 IMN at the tropopause.

Single-engine flying was also carried out to assess climb performance, the aircraft being set up in the landing configuration with one engine at idle thrust. BAC's recommendation that a single-engine climb-away speed of 175 kts IAS at 39,000 lb would give the optimum energy climb was confirmed. However, it was felt that this speed was too close to the stall to be practicable, and it was therefore recommended that single-engine climbs be made within the speed range 180–200 kts IAS at low altitude.

During the handling trials two instances of engine surge were experienced. The first incident occurred during a high IMN acceleration at 38,000 ft, the outside air temperature (OAT) being -61° C. Reheat was selected at 0.9 IMN with the intention of accelerating to 2.0 IMN, but at 1.9 IMN loud bangs were heard and reheat was cancelled. Reheat was then reselected and the acceleration continued to 2.0 IMN. Instrumentation records showed that on No. 2 engine there had been two comparatively minor compressor disturbances, followed by two larger ones at 1.94 and 1.95 IMN. On reheat being reselected, the jet pipe pressure recorded on No. 2 engine was very unstable and there were a number of indications of 'pop' surge between 1.85 and 2.0 IMN. An examination of the inlet guide vane angle/rpm relationship showed that, while on No. 1 engine the inlet guide vanes were working normally, those on No. 2 engine were at an angle 14 degrees more negative than the design value at the time the surges occurred. The second incident took place at 2,000 ft and involved malfunction of the nozzle.

A handling assessment of the F.6 with regard to flight refuelling was made using XP693 and Victor K.1 XA918. Wet and dry contacts were made on all three tanker stations at speeds from 245 to 270 kts IAS at 30,000 and 35,000 ft. Fuel states varied from full to 3,000 lb of fuel in the wing tanks, ventral tank empty. Although it was recommended in the

F.3 CA release that autostabilizers should not be used during formation flying, it was considered satisfactory to use these during flight refuelling, since it could be shown that there was sufficient control authority and time available to correct the attitude and position of the aircraft in the event of autostabilizer malfunction. Some contacts were made with the autostabilizers switched off, but it proved to be a significantly more difficult operation than with them on.

The Lightning F.6 behaved similarly to previous marks during flight refuelling, but it was noticeably less affected by changes in weight and speed. At the lower speed of 250 kts IAS its handling characteristics were significantly better than the F.2. For refuelling the 'stand-off' technique was used whereby the aircraft was positioned 4–6 ft behind the probe before a slight power increase moved the aircraft slowly forwards until contact was made. With full fuel the maximum practical height for refuelling was about 35,000 ft, at which point 95 per cent rpm on both engines was required for steady flight, leaving 5 per cent in reserve for station keeping. The use of reheat was also investigated, but selection on one engine only still resulted in excessive acceleration, so that the aircraft was likely to overshoot the drogue.

Although little difficulty was experienced in making a successful contact with the centre drogue, both the wing drogues presented steadier targets and were generally easier to make contact with. As the tanker was approached the effect of downwash from its wing tended to roll the Lightning towards the tanker, although the stick forces could easily be trimmed out. Contacts, station keeping and withdrawals were all found to be easy to achieve.

Further trials with the Lightning F.6 led to the publication of Pilot's Notes, a comprehensive manual that described the aircraft's various systems, performance and handling characteristics, together with flight limitations, emergency procedures and operating data. High-speed flight in the F.6 was described as follows:

> The aircraft is capable of exceeding its airspeed and Mach number limitations of 650 kts/2.0 M and care must be taken to avoid flying beyond these limits. Mach number must not exceed 1.3 M with airbrakes out.
>
> The aircraft is subject to intake vibration and intake buzz. Vibration occurs with the engines at full power at speeds above 1.88 M and may also occur within the range 1.35–1.60 M; it is due to turbulence of the airflow behind the intake bullet. It is felt as a low amplitude vibration similar to aerodynamic buffet and is structurally acceptable to the aircraft.
>
> Intake buzz is caused by a more violent disruption of the

airflow in the intake and will occur if the engines are throttled rapidly at speeds above 1.85 M. With increased 'g', buzz will occur at a lower Mach number and at higher rpm. It is indicated by a series of loud and rapidly recurrent bangs. The condition will not persist because with application of 'g' or on throttling back, the aircraft will decelerate rapidly beyond the buzz boundary. Intake buzz causes no damage but should be avoided.

During accelerations near the tropopause, longitudinal trim changes vary slightly with missile configuration. Generally there is a slight nose-down trim change as speed is increased from 0.90 to 0.98 M; there is no change of trim between 0.98 and 1.1 M but above this speed the trim change is very slightly nose-up, continuing progressively to approximately 1.4 M. There is no noticeable trim change above 1.4 M.

With only one missile fitted, there is a pronounced directional change of trim with change of speed. At 10,000 ft the rudder trimmer authority is adequate, but at 40,000 ft an increasing pedal force may be required above 1.7 M.

In transonic flight care must be taken when using large tailplane deflections. As Mach number is increased supersonically, aircraft response to tailplane movement decreases. Nevertheless care should be taken when applying 'g' rapidly, particularly at high fuel states and above 1.8 M where the lower 'g' limitations can more easily be exceeded.

The handling characteristics change appreciably in the region 1.2–1.4 M above 550 kts, particularly when missiles are fitted and when 'g' is applied. In this region application of aileron induces pronounced adverse yaw, causing reduced roll response and a feeling of heaviness. Difficulty may be experienced in accurate trimming, therefore rudder co-ordination is important during all manoeuvres.

On some aircraft, at supersonic speed, an increasing directional trim change may occur with increasing speed. This will require repeated applications of rudder trim as Mach number is increased; the trimmer should only be used, however, if sideslip exceeds half-ball width.

Airbrake operation at high speed causes a slight nose-down trim change and mild buffet. Directional stability is reduced with airbrakes extended, hence the more severe limitations in this configuration.

Below 10,000 ft control is affected as follows – above about 400 kts, longitudinal stick forces are light and care must be taken to observe 'g' limitations. The effect is more pronounced at low fuel states or if the autostabilizers are switched off. Above about 600 kts, nose-down trimmer authority is inadequate and the tailplane is near its forward limit. It is recommended that the autopilot master switch is left on, otherwise the autostabilizer actuator will drift to one end of its restricted stroke and thus may reduce the tailplane angle available by 1 degree. On some aircraft there may be a slight lateral trim change at approximately 0.97 M.

The flight and engine limitations for the Lightning F.6 were as follows:

Airframe Limitation – Maximum Speeds

With or without missiles	2.0 M/650 kts
With overwing tanks	0.95 M (0.9 M with single missile)/475 kts
Airbrake operation	1.3 M/650 kts
Undercarriage selection	250 kts
With undercarriage down	280 kts (in emergency)
Flap operation	250 kts
Parachute stream	160 kts (normal) 175 kts (emergency) – Mk.2
	170 kts (normal) 190 kts (emergency) – Mk.3

Minimum Speeds

Flaps and undercarriage up	180 kts
Flaps and undercarriage down	140 kts

NB – maintain higher speeds with 'g' applied. Add 5 knots per 2,000 lb increase above 36,000 lb a.u.w.

'G' Limitations – Positive – Combat

	Ventral Pack Fuel				
	<2,500 lb/ side internal	>1,000 lb	1,000– 3,500 lb	3,500 lb+	Single missile
Up to 0.9 M	6 g	6 g	5.5 g	5 g	4 g
0.9–1.80 M	6 g	5.5 g	5 g	4.5 g	4 g
Above 1.8 M	4 g	4 g	4 g	4 g	4 g

'G' Limitations – Positive – Ferry

With two or no missiles	3.5 g with fuel in overwing tanks, or 4 g with overwing tanks empty
With single missile	2 g

'G' Limitations – Negative

All configurations and fuel states – 3 g (negative 'g' must not be applied for longer than 15 seconds)

Weight Limitations

Take-off (combat) 39,000 lb	Take-off (ferry) 45,000 lb
Landing (normal) 34,500 lb	Landing (emergency) 39,000 lb

Altitude Limitation

Maximum permitted 60,000 ft

Engine Limitations

Power Rating	Time Limit/ Flight (min)	rpm %	Max JPT (°C)
Max (with or without reheat)	15 (combined)	100.5 max	790
Intermediate	30	97.5 max	755
Max continuous	Unrestricted	95 max	720
Approach	Unrestricted	60 min	–
Slow idle	Unrestricted	31–34	700

CHAPTER ELEVEN

Stall/Spin Trials with the Lightning F.6

Although the Lightning was never cleared for intentional spinning, it was the subject of an intensive series of stall/spin trials carried out by the manufacturers and by service test pilots of the A&AEE. One such trial was carried out at Boscombe Down in March/April 1970 using XP697, the Lightning F.6 prototype. A re-fuelling probe was fitted throughout the testing period, and flights were made with and without Red Top missiles.

The trials were commenced with stalls from 1 g flight with the aircraft trimmed wings level at 0.9 IMN at 45,000 ft with throttles set to idle/fast idle. Speed was then progressively reduced at 1–2 kts per second. Aircraft characteristics noted during the deceleration were as follows:

220 kts	Level 46,000 ft
215 kts	Onset of moderate airframe buffet
185 kts	Gentle wing rock
180 kts	Slight increase in airframe buffet, descending at 1,000 ft/min
145 kts	Slight lateral oscillation
115 kts	Gentle yaw left, then right

Recovery was made by moving the stick to just forward of neutral and applying full cold power. During the deceleration moderate buffet had began suddenly at 215 kts IAS and changed very little with further reduction in speed. At 185 kts IAS a gentle wing rock was observed (±10 degrees angle of bank) and this ceased at 160 kts IAS. The aircraft was allowed to descend at this stage in order to maintain the slow deceleration. At 145 kts IAS a slight lateral oscillation gave the pilot a 'knife edge' feeling, but this again disappeared with further reduction in speed. At 115 kts IAS the aircraft yawed gently to the left, only to reverse quickly to the right at an increased rate. The aircraft also started to roll to the right up to approximately 60 degrees angle of bank before this was arrested by recovery action.

In common with earlier marks of Lightning, the pre-stall buffet warning and wing rocking were not sufficient to constitute an un-mistakeable stall warning, and it was felt that these could well pass unnoticed under operational conditions. The behaviour of the F.6 at the stall, however, was different from previous marks in that it possessed better longitudinal and directional stability, with the result that the tendency to 'yaw off' was greatly reduced. With missiles on, the rate of descent was approximately 2,000 ft/min with the control column fully back, although BAC had recorded sink rates of up to 6,000 ft/min. One stall was flown without missiles. Characteristics were generally similar, although on this occasion a slight tendency to stick force lightening was noted at 125 kts IAS.

The next step in the trial involved spins from 1 g flight. The aircraft was trimmed at 0.9 IMN at 45,000 ft with the throttles set to idle/fast idle and the airspeed gradually reduced. At 135 kts IAS full rudder was applied in the desired direction and the control column moved fully aft. Rudder forces were moderate, but both hands were required to move the stick to the fully aft position. It was also found that this technique helped to maintain the ailerons at neutral. With full rudder the aircraft immediately yawed gently in the direction of rudder application, the rate of yaw increasing markedly when the stick was moved back, together with a steady increase in the rate of roll. The nose of the aircraft also pitched up very gently before dropping below the horizon with the build-up in roll.

On completion of the first turn, the nose rose again slightly above the horizon, this being a good indication of the completion of the first turn. The nose then fell steeply during the second turn with the change of flight path from horizontal to vertical. Rates of roll and yaw remained fairly constant after the first half of the turn and averaged approxi-mately 70 degrees per second. This made the spin quite comfortable and stable. Height loss after the first turn was only 330–500 ft, increasing to 800–1,000 ft after the second turn. Although the pilot was initially forced to one side of the cockpit during spin entry, this quickly became less noticeable with the build-up in rate of roll. Spin characteristics were almost identical to port and starboard, the only slight difference occurring during spin entry. During spins to the right the entry was generally more flat, the aircraft yawing through 50–60 degrees before any roll occurred in the direction of the spin. Airbrakes had no noticeable effect on the spin and the additional height loss during recovery was minimal.

To recover, full opposite rudder was applied, which required only a moderate force, and this was followed by a stick movement to just forward of neutral. With full anti-spin controls applied the rate of yaw decreased markedly, but the rate of roll was slow to decrease. The very noticeable reduction in the yaw rate initially led to centralizing of the rudder at 100 kts IAS. With experience, however, full opposite rudder was maintained until 150 kts IAS, making the recovery very much more positive. During the recovery the rate of roll was slow to decrease and sometimes the aircraft was still rolling gently at 250 kts IAS. With the residual roll the aircraft invariably ended up in a steep vertical dive. Controlling the roll with aileron was delayed until 250 kts IAS to avoid the possibility of entering another spin. The aircraft always recovered within 1–1½ turns, and the height loss from the time rudder was centralized to level flight averaged 7,000 ft. The pull-out was made by allowing speed to build up to 270–300 kts IAS, which was maintained by pulling 3 g, full power being applied at the same time.

Spins to port from 1 g flight with missiles removed (faired pylons) showed some notable differences from those with the missiles in place, and were generally much more hesitant, with large variations in the rate of yaw. A deceleration was carried out as before with full left rudder being applied at 135 kts IAS, followed by full aft stick. The aircraft initially yawed gently to the left before a sudden and rapid build-up of yaw occurred. The pilot was forced to the right-hand side of the cockpit during this manoeuvre, before the roll built up to its maximum value. After approximately three quarters of a turn the rates of roll and yaw decreased quite markedly, and on completion of the first turn the nose of the aircraft was some 10 degrees above the horizon. The rate of yaw then built up rapidly again, followed by an equally rapid build-up in roll as the aircraft entered its second turn. As the spin was more oscillatory it was difficult to count the number of turns accurately. With the flight path changing from horizontal to vertical, the only way that turns could be counted with any degree of certainty was by reference to the horizon.

On completion of the second turn with the nose level with the horizon, full opposite rudder was applied, followed by a stick movement to just forward of neutral, maintaining ailerons neutral. The rate of yaw appeared to decrease less rapidly than when missiles were fitted and there was no tendency for the pilot to centralize the rudder too early. As speed built up steadily through 150 kts IAS the rudder was centralized with the aircraft in an 80-degree dive, still rolling to the left. Speed built up quite quickly as full cold power was applied, the rolling tendency being controlled by a small application of aileron at 250 kts IAS, followed by a 3 g pull-out, maintaining 270 kts IAS.

Spins to starboard were similar, but very oscillatory. The entry was a little more sudden, with a very rapid build-up in yaw followed by roll, with peak rates being achieved within the first quarter of the turn. The rate of rotation then decreased so that by completion of the first turn rotation had ceased completely. With full pro-spin controls the aircraft descended in a level attitude with wings level for 1–2 seconds before again suddenly yawing to the right. The second turn was almost identical to the first, rotation again ceasing on completion of the second turn. During the second hesitation, recovery action was taken by centralizing the rudder and moving the stick just forward of neutral. Power was then applied and the aircraft slowly accelerated in a 20-degree dive, wings level.

Spins were also entered from turning flight. The aircraft was trimmed at 0.95 IMN at 45,000 ft with full cold power selected and then put into a 60-degree banked turn in the required direction. As the speed fell through 200 kts IAS, the control column was moved fully aft, normal acceleration at this point typically being around 2½ g. Buffet and wing rocking (around ±5 degrees angle of bank) were similar to earlier marks of Lightning, but as in the 1 g stall the F.6 exhibited greater longitudinal and directional stability at high incidence and with Red Top missiles. As speed decreased the aircraft rolled slowly left, irrespective of the direction of turn (probably owing to the FR probe), and if full rearward control column movement was maintained, the nose yawed to port and the aircraft entered a spin. To some extent this contrasted with the experience of BAC, which had found that in several cases, even with rapid rearward movement of the stick, the aircraft did not flick or spin, but continued in a steep spiral dive with a very high rate of descent.

Application of aileron to reverse the turn direction just prior to the stall resulted in an immediate flick roll through up to 360 degrees in a direction away from the applied aileron. It was thought that an attempted turn reversal at low speed would undoubtedly be the primary trigger action of service spin accidents. In the majority of cases, centralizing the controls effected recovery from the incipient spin that resulted from this kind of manoeuvre.

The Lightning F.6 exhibited a greater tendency to 'flick roll' with the missiles removed, and if the spin was allowed to develop the 'controls central' recovery technique could not be relied upon. Instead, application of rudder was needed to oppose the direction of yaw, this producing an immediate recovery. During a spin to port (no missiles), when 10 degrees of right aileron was applied in an attempt to reverse the turn, the aircraft pitched up almost immediately and yawed viciously to the left. This particular manoeuvre was rather alarming for the pilot as it was not consistent with previous experience. In this case the roll rate also built up very rapidly, and roll and yaw rates of 90 and 80 degrees per second were achieved within the first quarter of a turn. As the aircraft settled into the spin, however, the rate of rotation decreased, the spin becoming oscillatory and very similar to that experienced from a straight stall entry.

Effects of controls were investigated during two recoveries. On the first, 5 degrees of inspin aileron was applied, which prompted the aircraft to recover very quickly, so quickly in fact that the actual point of recovery was missed and it flicked and entered a spin in the opposite direction (away from the applied aileron). During the second recovery 7 degrees of outspin aileron was applied, but on this occasion recovery was not effected. The effect of elevator was investigated during a reversed recovery, where the elevator was moved to just forward of neutral. This caused an immediate increase in the rate of rotation, the spin also becoming more stable. Full outspin rudder was then applied and recovery occurred within 9 seconds after about 2½ turns. With this high rate of rotation, which was estimated at 100 degrees per second, it was difficult to count the number of turns and it was possible for the pilot to suffer slight disorientation owing to the rapid changes in roll and yaw.

One of the greatest criticisms of the Lightning's stall/spin character-istics was the fact that it had virtually no stall warning and therefore no spin warning. The moderate airframe buffet that became evident at high incidence occurred at speeds well above the stall (around 215 kts IAS) and changed very little right down to the stall, which, depending on weight and configuration, took place at about 115 kts IAS. As the aircraft would have to be flown well within the buffet boundary in order to manoeuvre effectively during air combat, it would clearly be difficult for the pilot to know precisely how close to the stall he was. The only real warning was the 'yaw off' just before the flick or spin, but this was likely to be too late. Once the aircraft had flicked it would most probably end up in a spin, and it was thought that the average squadron pilot would be ill equipped to recover, in terms of both inexperience and lack of cockpit indication.

Several Lightnings were lost in service as a result of departures during air combat training, one of the first being F.6 XR766 of 23 Squadron on 7 September 1967. The aircraft was being flown by Sqn Ldr Ron Blackburn, and was acting as a target at 34,000 ft in a subsonic inter-ception exercise. To make the sortie as realistic as possible a hard evading turn to port was carried out using full cold power. When speed had reduced to 250 kts IAS, the nose of the aircraft was allowed to fall below the horizon and a downward aileron turn was performed. At 25,000 ft, at around 210 kts IAS, the wings were levelled and back pressure applied to the controls to reduce the rate of descent. At this point the nose lifted sharply and yawed to the right. The stick was immediately centralized but this did not prevent the aircraft from entering a spin to the left. The pilot took the normal spin recovery action but the aircraft failed to respond.

After 2–3 turns with the controls in the normal spin recovery position, full pro-spin controls were applied for two turns before full anti-spin controls were tried once again. Just as before, the Lightning showed no sign of recovery, and in an attempt to break the stability of the spin the pilot attempted alternate applications of full pro- and anti-spin aileron for a further four turns, but without success. By now the aircraft was down to around 8,000 ft, at which height Blackburn ejected, his machine continuing to spin until it hit the sea. He was rescued by helicopter an hour later. The accident report stated that the aircraft might have been saved if the controls had been held in the spin recovery position for longer than 2–3 turns, although there was nothing in Pilot's Notes at the time to suggest that this might be the case. A similar accident occurred on 28 January 1971 and involved F.2A XN772 of 92 Squadron, which crashed near Diepholz in Germany after entering a spin during an air combat exercise. The pilot, Flg Off Pete Hitchcock, ejected safely.

CHAPTER TWELVE

Accidents and Incidents

T he accident rate for the Lightning was no worse than any other comparable fighter aircraft, although the period 1970/1 saw a peak, with a total of seventeen aircraft lost. During its long career it was to suffer from a wide variety of accidents and incidents, and the following review looks at specific examples to illustrate some of the more common causes of these mishaps.

UNDERCARRIAGE PROBLEMS

In the early days of Lightning operations, undercarriage snags were a particular hazard, with any failure of the main landing gear leaving the pilot with no alternative but to abandon his aircraft. This situation occurred on 5 March 1960, when XG334 of AFDS had its port undercarriage leg jam halfway when the gear was selected down. Sqn Ldr Ron Harding tried everything he knew to lower the offending leg, but it was to no avail and he was eventually forced to eject over the sea. A large part of the port wing was recovered and sent to Warton for investigation, where it was concluded that the failure was most probably caused by an obstruction in the hydraulic pressure pipe caused by collapse of the inner damper tube. As a result of this accident strengthened damper tubes were incorporated.

Despite modifications, main gear failures continued to occur. Lightning F.1A XM185 of 56 Squadron was lost on 28 June 1961 when the undercarriage refused to lower following normal selection and 'emergency down'. Flt Lt Pete Ginger had no choice but to eject and did so safely near Lavenham in Suffolk. It was later considered that the failure was caused by a fatigue fracture of the hydraulic pressure service pipe. On 11 September 1964 Flt Lt Terry Bond of 226 OCU was carrying out an air test on F.1 XM134, which had previously shown a malfunction of the undercarriage indicator lights. The undercarriage was cycled three times successfully, but on the fourth selection the starboard leg did not fully extend. This was followed by a HYD 1 warning, which indicated failure of one of the hydraulic systems powering the flying controls. This system also provided power for the emergency operation of the undercarriage. Various manoeuvres were flown to apply 'g' loadings, but the leg still refused to move. With fuel running low Bond carried out a successful ejection off the coast of Norfolk near Happisburgh.

Flt Lt Dave Jones of 19 Squadron experienced a different sort of undercarriage problem on 15 October 1962 when flying Lightning F.2 XN774 from Leconfield:

> I was briefed and authorized for a routine radar training sortie and took off as No. 2 thirty seconds after my leader. The take-off was normal. However, at 200 ft the main wheels locked up but the nosewheel remained red. I climbed at 200 kts to 3,000 ft and selected undercarriage down, obtaining two mainwheel greens and a nosewheel red. I then turned downwind, called for a GCA as the cloud base was about 900 ft and flew past the tower. They informed me that the nosewheel was up but that the doors appeared to be open.
>
> I then climbed back up to 3,000 ft and selected undercarriage up, the main wheels retracted normally, but again the nosewheel remained red. During and after all the selections the services HYD pressure remained normal and the situation did not change even after the application of positive and negative 'g'. When the fuel was 1,800/1,800 lb I selected emergency undercarriage down with negative 'g' and then maintained positive 'g' (3½) at 320 kts without effect. I continued to pull and push 'g' at speeds between 180 and 320 kts and carried out a roller landing, but still there was no change.
>
> I flew out to sea and jettisoned the ventral tank at 3,500 ft – this left the aircraft cleanly at 250 kts with little change of trim. I then returned to the airfield and jettisoned the canopy at 220 kts at 200 ft with flaps up. It appeared to leave the aircraft very cleanly with a loud 'pop', and I was later told that the canopy missed the fin by about six feet. There was little disturbance in the cockpit without the hood and it was very similar to driving an open-top sports car. I was able to raise the seat for landing without any problems. The landing was carried out with 600 lb fuel and I held the nose in the air and lowered it gently onto the runway at about 75 kts. Pitch control was positive down to this speed. The aircraft

came to rest in the middle of the pre-prepared foam strip and stopped in about 1,200 yards.

It was subsequently discovered that the starboard 'pip-pin' that retained the nosewheel door strut had become detached and during the retraction sequence had penetrated the inner surface of the rear door, forming a lock across the shimmy damper assembly. A spot check carried out on all other Lightning aircraft in service found four with the pins partially withdrawn. For his calm and professional handling of the emergency, Dave Jones was awarded a Green Endorsement in his logbook. He was not the last to be confronted with a two-wheeled landing, Flg Off Ian MacFadyen successfully landed F.1 XM144 at Coltishall on 29 September 1964, and F.2 XN783 landed in similar fashion at Leconfield on 16 November 1965.

Two accidents occurred on Lightning T.4s because of imperfections in the casting of undercarriage legs, the most dramatic being XM993 of the Lightning Conversion Squadron (LCS) at Middleton St George on 12 December 1962. Shortly after touchdown Flt Lt Al Turley, and his student, Wg Cdr Charles Gibbs, became aware that the port wing was beginning to drop. Suspecting that a tyre had burst, and with the aircraft veering towards the edge of the runway, Turley applied full starboard rudder and brake in an attempt to keep the Lightning straight, but it soon became apparent that the port undercarriage had collapsed. Before coming to rest, the aircraft slewed 90 degrees to port and then rolled to starboard, breaking its fuselage as it did so. Although fire broke out, both pilots escaped unhurt. (Turley was involved in another emergency on 24 August 1966, when he was forced to eject from F.3 XP760 over the North Sea following an engine fire.) Although not of the same magnitude, a similar incident occurred at Binbrook on 22 January 1963, when XM973 of AFDS suffered a collapsed starboard undercarriage leg when lining up for take-off.

There were also problems with the undercarriage side-stay brackets on Lightning F.1s, which caused the demise of two development-batch aircraft, XG311 and XG335. English Electric test pilot Don Knight ejected from the former over the Ribble Estuary on 31 July 1963, and Sqn Ldr A.J. Whittaker abandoned XG335 over the Larkhill ranges in Wiltshire on 11 January 1965.

Engine Fires and Fire Warnings

In 1970/1 there was a worrying escalation in the number of Lightning accidents, the majority of which were caused by in-flight fires. The situation got so bad that serious questions were asked about the validity of the Lightning force as numbers were dwindling at an alarming rate. As part of the deliberations on the Lightning a survey was carried out in early 1971 to try to put the aircraft's accident rate into some sort of perspective. From its entry into service in July 1960 there had been 110 accidents, resulting in forty write-offs. It was found that fires had caused the largest percentage in both categories – thirty-three accidents and fifteen write-offs (30 and 37.5 per cent respectively). When broken down by marks, the F.1/1A, F.3 and F.6 accounted for 82 per cent of all accidents through fire, with the F.3 alone being responsible for 33 per cent. Although these figures were bad enough, the overall write-off rate was comparable with both the Javelin and Hunter. The Lightning was on a par with the Javelin in all respects, and although its overall accident rate was similar to the Hunter, there was a marked disparity between the two as regards the cause of these accidents. A Lightning was four times more likely to suffer an in-flight fire, but its accident rate as a result of pilot error was twice as good.

Particular emphasis was placed on the period January 1970 to May 1971, and it was found that most fire incidents occurred during the climb and under cruise/combat conditions, two aspects of flight involving higher power settings with correspondingly higher temperatures within the fire zones. Three-quarters of all real fire warnings were associated with the No. 1 (lower) engine, with hot gas leaks occurring in equal numbers on each engine installation. Spurious fire warnings were more likely to be associated with the No. 2 engine, giving rise to Fire 2 and Reheat 2 fire warnings in similar numbers. Real fires in the air were mostly caused by fuel leaks and hydraulic oil. Although a Fire Integrity Programme had been initiated in the late 1960s, it was discovered that of the nineteen fire accidents/incidents in 1971, fourteen occurred to aircraft that had been modified to minimize the occurrence of an in-flight fire. Fires also occurred on the ground, mainly during start up, the chief causes being Avpin and fuel venting. The level of pilot risk was also assessed, and assuming a four-year tour with 320 sorties per year (20 hours per month), the chances of a pilot experiencing an in-flight fire leading to abandonment was estimated to be 6 per cent, with subsequent risk of mortality at 1.5 per cent.

The RAF's first Lightning loss through fire occurred on 16 December 1960, and involved XM138 of AFDS. Flt Lt Bruce Hopkins was carrying out a practice interception at 36,000 ft when he felt a heavy airframe thump and a sudden jerk on the rudder pedals. At the same time a warning light illuminated and the AI scope went off line. During a GCA descent Hopkins was aware of an elevator restriction when the stick was moved back, but he was able to make a successful landing at Coltishall, during which the runway controller noticed fuel streaming from the aircraft. By the time the aircraft reached the end of the runway it was obvious that it was on fire, and extensive damage was caused to the rear fuselage before the flames were extinguished. An investigation revealed that the accident was primarily caused by rupture of the No. 1 engine exhaust cone, which permitted a hot gas leak to contact the starboard fire extinguisher bottle, which then burst violently. In doing so it damaged a fuel pipe, thereby releasing fuel into the hot engine bay, which then ignited.

Not long afterwards, Wattisham had its first fire emergency when Sqn Ldr (later AM Sir) John Rogers, OC 56 Squadron, received a Reheat 1 fire indication shortly after take-off in XM176 on 14 February 1961. A successful landing was made, but on shutting down No. 2 engine, smoke was seen coming from the rear fuselage. It was found that a fire had occurred between Frames 48 and 50 in the bottom of the fuselage and that this had caused Cat 3 damage. By coincidence a similar accident occurred at Warton two days later, involving XM181. The area of carbon deposit and torching appeared to be almost identical in that it was located directly above a drain hole in the fuselage, but in this case it was adjacent to Frame 52 instead of Frame 48. From all the evidence it was considered that the fires in both aircraft had been started by the ignition of hydraulic fuel (DTD 585) and AVTAG after contact with the No. 1 intermediate jet pipe assembly owing to unsatisfactory drainage from the fuselage and the top of the ventral tank.

As if to emphasize the fact that fires were more likely to occur when the engines were operating at high power settings, 74 Squadron experienced an emergency with XM140 on 3 April 1963 shortly after take-off. A Fire 1 warning occurred, which remained after power was reduced, and so the pilot descended below cloud while completing the appropriate fire drills. The ventral tank was jettisoned over open ground and the fire warning light went out at the end of the downwind leg that preceded an uneventful landing. It was established that the fire was caused by a fuel leak into the rear of the No. 1 engine bay, where it was ignited by radiated heat from the exhaust unit. It was thought that fuel had seeped through as a result of foreign matter becoming trapped between a fuel pipe and its union, even though the union was correctly tightened and locked.

In some cases an engine fire could lead to a titanium fire, and this occurred with F.6 XR773 of 74 Squadron at Tengah on 22 February 1968. During an approach to land the pilot reported a serious vibration and noticed that the No. 1 engine rpm was dropping rapidly, together with a corresponding rise in JPT. He then heard a 'positive clank', assumed that the engine had seized and closed the HP and LP cocks. JPT then reduced, and as there had been no audio or visual warning he assumed there was no fire. Shortly after landing, however, large quantities of white smoke issued from the air intake and the No. 1 engine jet pipe, and flames were seen in the region of the ventral tank.

Examination of the engine revealed that a titanium fire had occurred in the rear stages of the compressor, damaging most of the engine beyond repair. The fire had not been contained within the engine as fifteen holes had been burned in the compressor casings. The primary cause of the fire had been a fatigue failure of one of the Stage 5 stator blades caused by the high stresses experienced, and this had led to severe secondary damage. Although there had been four other failures of a Stage 5 stator blade in the Avon 301 in service, this was the first confirmed case of a titanium fire. As a result of this incident, Avon Mod 3497 introduced steel blades for stator Stages 5 and 6 instead of titanium, to reduce blade deflection and increase fatigue life. (XR773 survived the experience and is currently the only F.6 still flying, with Mike Beachy Head in South Africa.)

Sadly not all in-flight fires were survivable, and on 12 September 1968 Flt Lt P.F. Thompson of 74 Squadron was killed when F.6 XS896 (call-sign Mission 59) went out of control shortly before landing. Thompson was flying as No. 2 to Sqn Ldr Peter Carter, OC 'A' Flight, who recalled the sequence of events in his report:

> I was leader of a pair for a reheat take-off, cold power climb to FL 360, practice interception under Gombak control at or around FL 360 against subsonic targets, a pairs letdown to Point Alpha (18 miles from touchdown on the extended centreline of Tengah's runway) and finally, depending on fuel, either a pairs GCA to land or a pairs run in and break for landing.
>
> We took off in close formation at 1100 hrs and the sortie was flown without incident to Point Alpha. At this stage I asked Mission 59 for a fuel check and his reply, 'Joker plus 100', signified he had 2,500 lb remaining. As this fuel was sufficient for a pairs GCA and overshoot into the circuit, I elected to do this and declared my intention to ATC and to Mission 59. A normal GCA was flown and a standard pairs overshoot initiated from the runway threshold. I increased power to 90 per cent rpm in cruise nozzles on both engines, called and selected in turn, dive brakes in, wheels up, flaps up, and as the speed increased through 250 kts, called and executed a reduction in power to 87 per cent on both engines. We changed frequency to Local Control and, at the end of the runway, started a climbing turn on to the down-wind leg, using 40–45 degrees bank at 250–260 kts.
>
> At about 1,000 ft, with about 30 degrees to go to the runway

reciprocal, 59 disappeared from the view in my mirror and made an RT call that I understood to be, 'I have Reheat Fire 1 and 2 captions illuminated'. He said that he was turning underneath and inside me, so I selected maximum cold power and cleared his path high and to the right. I transmitted a Mayday call on local frequency and asked the tower to confirm that they were aware of the emergency.

From my position above and slightly ahead of 59, I checked his aircraft for signs of fire and saw none. 59 made an RT call indicating that he intended to land and I instructed him to stopcock both engines when on the runway. I then watched him fly what appeared to be a normal downwind leg. At the point where I would have expected him to start his finals turn, I saw the aircraft start to roll. It rolled through nearly 360 degrees and entered . . . a flat, upright spin to the left. I saw that the wheels were down and had the impression that the flaps also were in the down position. As soon as he entered the spin, I shouted over the RT, 'Get Out! Get Out! Get Out!' The spin continued for at least two turns before I saw the canopy separate from the aircraft. I then saw the seat leave the aircraft and both drogues deploy. The aircraft struck the ground and the seat and drogue-chutes entered the trees at a shallow angle very soon afterwards and only a short distance away. I saw no sign of the pilot separating from the seat.

The engineering report stated that XS896 had struck the ground with a low forward speed in a near horizontal attitude, but with a high rate of descent. A fire had developed in the air long enough before impact to burn through the control tube sleeve, thereby disconnecting the pilot's controls. This crash was similar to one that had occurred in 1962 in which de Havilland test pilot George Aird had ejected at very low level after control had been lost prior to landing at Hatfield. As a result of this accident Mod 2537 had replaced alloy control tubes with stainless steel, but in the case of XS896 it was felt that the fire most probably melted the light alloy internal sleeve of the joint in the stainless steel tubing.

By 1971 questions were being asked of the fueldraulic systems in the Lightning, with particular emphasis on the high pressures involved and the failure of gaskets. To reinforce these concerns Lightning F.6 XS938, flown by Flg Off Scott McLean, was lost on 28 April 1971 shortly after take-off from Leuchars. Just as the aircraft was reaching climbing speed the audio warning and visual attention-getters operated and the Fire 2 warning caption illuminated. Almost immediately the Reheat 2 warning was seen and the pilot carried out a full fire drill on the No. 2 engine. When turning back to base the Fire 2 caption went out but was replaced by a Reheat 1 warning. After levelling the wings and raising the nose, McLean ejected from the aircraft and was rescued, uninjured, from the sea by helicopter. From the wreckage that was recovered, the evidence pointed to a high-pressure fuel spray originating from the No. 2 engine fueldraulic system. The No. 2 fueldraulic pump was eventually found, and this revealed that a portion of the gasket at the connection between the pump and the flexible fuel flange was missing. It was concluded that the failure of the sealed joint was as a result of an insufficiently tightened flange nut adjacent to the point of failure of the gasket.

Unfortunately much of the evidence of the engine fire epidemic of 1970/1 ended up at the bottom of the sea, including that from F.3 XP705, whose final resting place was 6,500 ft below the surface of the Mediterranean off Akrotiri in Cyprus. On 8 July 1971 Flt Lt Graham Clarke of 29 Squadron was tasked to fly two consecutive air combat sorties with a quick turn-round between each. On the second sortie he was one of a pair for a 'yo-yo' exercise at 20,000 ft. The first manoeuvre to be carried out involved two 360-degree turns to the right, and on repeating this to the left Clarke descended to 16,000 ft with speed falling to 250 kts IAS. He then engaged full reheat to regain altitude, turned to port and on passing the second aircraft on a reciprocal heading, demonstrated an escape manoeuvre by levelling the wings, pushing the control column forward to apply zero 'g' for maximum acceleration.

After 2–3 seconds of zero 'g' Clarke heard what appeared to be an explosion and then felt the aircraft 'kick'. Shortly afterwards the audio warning sounded and the Reheat 1 fire warning illuminated. A full reheat fire drill was performed, a Mayday call was transmitted and about a minute later a restriction in the fore-and-aft movement of the controls was detected. Although the aircraft continued to respond normally to control movements, there was unmistakable stiffening in the pitching plane. A second audio alarm then denoted a Reheat 2 fire warning, which prompted Clarke to eject. The pilot of the accompanying aircraft saw it spiral steeply downwards trailing grey smoke from the No. 1 jet pipe to crash in the sea. Clarke suffered no injuries and was picked up by an SAR helicopter.

Although by the mid-1970s the prevalence of engine fires was much reduced, the risk was still very real. In June 1981 Brian Carroll experienced a reheat fire warning when flying a Lightning T.55 in Saudi Arabia:

A new course of Saudi students had nearly completed their ground-school training and were looking forward to their first taste of the 'Real Thing'. This was always known as the

'Instructor's Benefit Ride', since the student was assigned to the right-hand seat and simply had to sit back and enjoy the ride while the instructor demonstrated the full envelope of the aircraft. The briefing covered a reheat take-off and climb to 36,000 ft; turn performance in cold and in full reheat; a supersonic dash to around Mach 1.5; high rate descent to 2,000 ft (the rate of descent could easily reach 50,000 ft/min); low speed handling in the region of 200 kts with the undercarriage lowered; level accelera-tion at 2,000 ft to 600 kts pulling into a reheat, near vertical climb, aiming to level out at 36,000 ft followed by a standard recovery to base for a couple of circuits and a landing.

Initially, all went to plan, the student being duly impressed. We had just entered the vertical climb, following the maximum rate low level acceleration, when the Reheat 1 fire warning light came on and the audible warning sounded loudly in our earphones. Both reheats were immediately cancelled and No. 1 engine closed down with No. 2 at idle as we levelled at about 22,000 ft. Full emergency drills were completed and a Mayday call to Dhahran was made. We were some 80 miles SSW of base and at our present height we could glide with one engine at idle for approximately 55 to 60 miles. That would place us reasonably close to base should things deteriorate and force us to bale out. During the preceding few minutes, my student had calmly opened his emergency flip card, which, considering this was his first ride in a Lightning, was very commendable. He then asked if all the necessary actions had been taken. Working on the basis that one should never assume, but always check, we then went through them again to make sure that nothing had been omitted. Needless to say, nothing had. The student then asked what we should do. My response was, 'Do Not Panic'.

Our recovery continued towards Dhahran in a slow glide, maintaining sufficient power to keep the AC supplies on line (the AC power ran the main flight instruments). At around 8,000 ft the Reheat warning light was still on and a bale-out was looking ever more likely. Nine minutes (it seemed more like nine hours) after the warning illuminated, it finally went out. We were now over the Gulf on a straight-in approach with some 45 miles to go to touchdown. The flying controls continued to function normally and I decided that a landing was possible, though we were both ready to eject should the controls show any sign of stiffening. A high approach path was set up to give a little more height advan-tage should the situation deteriorate further. With eight miles still to go, I lowered the undercarriage and started the final approach.

At this moment the main flight instruments began to fail (not a good sign). AC power was then lost and we were close to flying on the proverbial wing and a prayer. At three miles the standby instruments also started to fail and just before touchdown all the electrics quit. The landing was uneventful and I allowed the aircraft to roll to the end of the runway where the remaining engine was switched off and, with the assistance of the fire crew, we both vacated the cockpit.

On inspection, the rear end of the aircraft was still burning, molten metal dripping on to the hard standing (I still own an engraved key fob made from one of the droplets of metal). The aircraft was declared Cat 3+, about as close as it could be to a complete write-off. 182 days later I flew this aircraft again on an Air Test following a near total rebuild. Two sorties, totalling 1 hr 30 min, proved the aircraft to be fully serviceable again, a credit to our engineers. My student successfully completed the course and was posted off to a base on the West Coast of Arabia. They say that lightning (no pun intended) never strikes twice, but in his case the prophets were going to be proved wrong. He had a repeat experience in a Lightning F.53, a Reheat 1 fire plus all the rest, a situation virtually identical to that encountered on his first ever trip. He landed successfully, and when I spoke to him over the phone and asked him about it he said, 'Sir, I Did Not Panic!'

The possibility of an in-flight fire was to remain the Lightning pilot's No. 1 concern right until the end of its operational career. Indeed, the last Lightning to be lost (F.6 XR769) went down over the North Sea on 11 April 1988 following a fire in the No. 1 engine bay. Flt Lt Dick Coleman, an Australian Mirage IIIO pilot on an exchange posting with 11 Squadron, ejected at 300 kts and 10,000 ft and was rescued by an ASR Wessex from Leconfield.

FIN FAILURES

The very first Lightning to be lost in an accident was the T.4 prototype (XL628) which broke up over the Irish Sea on 1 October 1959. On this occasion the aircraft was being flown by English Electric test pilot Johnny Squier, who had been tasked with investigating rolling stability at 1.7 M, the highest Mach number so far attempted. Squier's subsequent report relates the sequence of events:

After take-off the aircraft was climbed to 35,000 ft at 0.9 M with maximum reheat and an acceleration was then carried out up to

1.7 M at this height. During the course of the acceleration, records were taken of engine rpm and fuel contents. When reaching 1.7 M the aircraft was climbed up to 40,000 ft; during the course of this short climb it was noticed that the throttles had slipped back to Stage 3 so were reselected to maximum reheat. 40,000 ft was reached at 1.6 M and the aircraft was accelerated to 1.7 M at which point the Hussenots (recorders) were switched on and a maximum starboard roll initiated. All went well for the first three-quarters of the roll; however, just after passing the 270-degree mark the aircraft commenced to yaw violently. The amplitude of the yaw was approximately ten times as great as anything previously experienced under similar circumstances. As the yaw built up there was suddenly a loud 'crump' and immediately the aircraft yawed or spun directionally through a very large amplitude and at the same time flicked over and then appeared to yaw violently the other way and flick again in the opposite direction.

It was immediately realized that a form of structural failure had occurred and it was decided that there was only one thing to do and that was to bale out. As I raised my hands to get to the blind, I noticed that the probe had bent back and was lying across the intake at an angle of about 45 degrees to starboard. I pulled the blind handle firmly straight down and held it there. After a small period of time there was the 'woomph' of the canopy coming off, followed by a terrific bang as the seat fired. I have no recollection of hitting a violent slipstream or of excessive buffeting, but I was aware that I was spinning and eventually my hands were pulled off the blind handle by centrifugal force and flung out in a spread-eagle manner. The spinning was about the horizontal axis, looking upwards at the sky, and the rate of rotation was very high, leading to excruciating pain in my arm sockets.

After a momentary flick, the motion stopped and I was then hanging forward in a slightly face-forward attitude, which is the normal attitude for a descent in a Martin-Baker seat with the drogue extended. After what appeared to be an almost interminable period of time, there was a sudden 'clang' and my legs dropped, and on looking up it seemed that the seat had come away and had gone upwards. After falling for a further period of time waiting for the parachute to open, it suddenly dawned on me that it should have appeared when the seat left, so I pulled the manual ring. There was an immense feeling of deceleration and shortly after I hit the water and went straight down, apparently to a great depth. I pulled the inflation knob of my Mae West and was hauled back to the surface once again.

Squier managed to inflate his dinghy and was washed up on the coast of Galloway 24 hours later. Although not badly injured, it proved to be the end of his career as a test pilot. Despite initial suggestions that there might have been inadvertent selection of undercarriage or airbrakes, the accident was eventually proved to have been caused by fin failure as a result of inertia coupling. This phenomenon affected many high-speed fighter projects of the period, those featuring a long, heavy body mated to relatively short-span wings. In the case of the Lightning the vertical tail surfaces were enlarged and strengthened and strict rolling limitations were imposed. Even so the first T.5 (XM966) was lost on 22 July 1965 during rapid rolling trials with the 2 in rocket pack extended. Once again the aircraft had suffered fin failure caused by the effects of roll coupling, pilot Jimmy Dell and flight test observer G. Elkington both ejecting safely.

Structural failures of the fin/rudder occurred on several other occasions, although in these instances the causes were entirely different. The most spectacular took place on 16 May 1961 and involved a member of 74 Squadron's aerobatic team. During a low-level formation run at around Mach 0.97 the rudder and a substantial part of the fin of XM141 broke away. Flt Lt Jim Burns was able to land without further incident, and it was later concluded that the accident had been caused by aerodynamic interaction between the aircraft flying in close proximity at high subsonic Mach number at low altitude. This had significance not only for formation aerobatics, but also operationally, in particular the need to fly in close formation for cloud penetration. Following a prolonged investigation various limitations were imposed in terms of IMN/IAS, normal acceleration and lateral separation between aircraft when in formation.

Slightly less catastrophic failures occurred on a number of other occasions. Lightning T.4 XM972 of 226 OCU lost its rudder on 7 March 1967 but was recovered safely to Coltishall, and F.6 XR771 suffered similar damage on 16 August 1972. In the latter incident the pilot was descending at 0.98 M/620 kts IAS after carrying out a high-speed practice interception when he felt a vibration that lasted about two seconds. The aircraft felt sluggish in the circuit, and on landing with a slight crosswind he was unable to keep straight without the use of brake. On arrival back at dispersal the rudder was seen to be missing and it was later surmised that there had been a fatigue failure of the upper hinge assembly.

BRAKING PARACHUTE FAILURES

In the early 1960s problems were regularly experienced on landing with frequent failure of the braking parachute. Although on a dry runway braking action should have been sufficient to stop the aircraft by the upwind end of the runway, less than ideal conditions and/or inadequate braking led to a number of barrier engagements. One such incident occurred on 18 December 1962 and involved Lightning F.2 XN777 of AFDS. After a normal landing, the pilot applied the brakes for a functional check prior to streaming the brake chute. The runway was wet and there was a 12–15 kt crosswind component. The parachute deployed but, unbeknown to the pilot, candled almost immediately. Braking did not prevent the aircraft going into the barrier, which was extended nearly 600 ft, the Lightning coming to rest beyond the airfield boundary with its nosewheel and strut buried in a ploughed field. The upper barrier cable had cut into the spine of the aircraft and both main oleos were damaged by the lower cable.

Barrier engagements could cause considerable damage, in particular to the fuselage spine, which was the case with F.1 XM145 of 74 Squadron on 19 August 1963. Following failure of the brake chute, the pilot overshot before making a precautionary landing. Although the landing was good, there was little braking action in the last 1,000 yards of the runway, leading to contact with the barrier, the top cable of which raked along the aircraft's spine, rupturing the Avpin tank, which was set on fire. The pilot successfully evacuated the aircraft but severe damage was caused to electrical equipment, rendering the aircraft Cat 3. Examination of the rigging lines showed that twelve had been severed, causing the parachute to collapse, and there was also evidence of extensive brake pad wear, indicative of a previous 'hot-stop' landing.

LOST CANOPIES

During early testing of the P.1A there had been a worrying tendency for the canopy to depart in flight, a situation that had occurred on three separate occasions. A revised canopy locking system proved to be the cure. A number of canopies were also lost in service, although in these cases the cause was usually failure on the part of the pilot to check that it was properly locked prior to take-off. The F.2 appeared to be particularly prone to this type of accident, the first occurring on 24 September 1964. A 92 Squadron pilot was about to fly his first solo conversion exercise in an F.2 (XN793) but forgot to secure the canopy, probably as a result of being distracted by an RT problem. On take-off the canopy broke away and hit the tailplane, causing damage to the leading edge of the fin.

A similar incident occurred on 6 August 1965, involving XN776 of 19 Squadron. The pilot partially opened his canopy for ventilation while waiting to line up and forgot to lock it before take-off. Like the previous occasion, the canopy hit the fin as it left the aircraft. 19 Squadron did it again on 21 February 1966 when pilot distraction again contributed to the loss of a canopy from XN775. Not to be outdone, 111 Squadron got in on the act on 18 July 1966 when F.3 XP741 lost its canopy on take-off, failure to complete the pre-take-off checks being the prime cause. Treble One had lost another canopy in slightly different fashion on 23 June 1964 when T.4 XM992 was due to form part of an eight-aircraft scramble as part of an exercise. The pilot was delayed as a result of being unable to start No. 2 engine, and jet blast from the other aircraft, which were taking off in close proximity, ripped off the T.4's canopy, causing damage to the hinge mechanisms.

TAKE-OFF ACCIDENTS

It was possible for incidents to occur as a result of handling differences between the various marks of Lightning. The take-off technique with the F.6 required the selection of flap, a lot of aft stick to raise the nosewheel, followed by a check forward when airborne to prevent an excessive rate of climb. The F.3, however, was taken off without the use of flap and did not need quite so much back stick and consequently no check forward. On one occasion a first-tour pilot, who had become accustomed to the F.6, was required to fly a sortie in an F.3. After lifting off at 175 kts IAS he selected undercarriage up but noticed that the airspeed had stabilized at 180 kts IAS and the aircraft was not climbing as it should. Instead it began to descend, and the ventral tank, containing 1,700 lb of fuel, touched the runway. The pilot engaged reheat on both engines and eventually managed to get his aircraft to climb, but this also served to ignite fuel escaping through a hole in the ventral tank. Despite severe damage to the underside and tailplane, a safe landing was made, the Lightning being declared Cat. 3. As there was nothing technically wrong with the aircraft it was thought that the pilot had instinctively used his F.6 technique on take-off and had unwittingly prevented it from taking off in the normal manner.

This incident was similar to one that occurred to a Lightning F.3 (XP700) on 7 August 1972 during a five-aircraft stream take-off. The pilot took off and retracted the undercarriage but his aircraft sank back onto the runway, where the ventral tank remained in contact with the ground for some 500 yards, before finally becoming airborne. A heavy fuel leak from the ventral tank caused a fierce fire and the pilot shut down the No. 2 engine when he received a Reheat 2 fire warning. The controls began to stiffen and shortly afterwards there was a controls hydraulic failure, at which point the pilot ejected. He landed safely, but with back injuries.

Both of the aircraft mentioned above at least managed to get into the air, which was not the case on 29 October 1971 when a pilot of 111 Squadron was attempting to take off in F.3 XR711. Part of a three-ship stream take-off, he applied full cold power before selecting reheat and noted that all engine indications were normal. Just before the calculated lift-off point the aircraft touched its tail bumper and ventral fin on the runway, leaving a mark some 50 ft long. The aircraft skipped for a further 50 ft before settling onto the ventral tank and bursting into flames (the undercarriage having been selected up at some time just before the first mark on the runway). The aircraft continued to slide on its belly down the remaining 4,700 ft of runway. For the most part it stayed level, although at one point the port wing tip scraped the ground, and gradually it settled forward onto its nose. By this time burning fuel from the ruptured ventral tank was spilling onto the runway and continued to burn on the surface. The aircraft entered the barrier at high speed, breaking the bottom cable, the top cable remaining to cut a deep groove in the base of the fin. It finally came to rest some 500 ft past the barrier, whereupon the pilot, who was unhurt, quickly vacated the cockpit.

This was not the first time that 111 Squadron had lost an aircraft during a stream take-off, as XR714 went into the barrier in similar circumstances at Akrotiri on 27 September 1966. On this occasion the pilot was No. 4 in a four-aircraft formation but experienced severe wake turbulence from preceding aircraft, to the extent that his strip speed ASI began to fluctuate. He therefore had to rely on his standby ASI up to 120 kts IAS, by which time the strip ASI was working correctly again. Shortly after becoming airborne, with the undercarriage retracted, severe turbulence was again experienced and the pilot was unable to prevent the port wing dropping. The aircraft sank back onto the runway and engaged the barrier, sustaining Cat 4 damage in the process.

LANDING ACCIDENTS

Throughout the Lightning's service career a number of accidents occurred on landing. One of the most impressive 'arrivals' occurred on 19 November 1963 when Lightning F.1A XM187 of 111 Squadron was making a night landing after several practice interceptions. The aircraft touched down heavily and bounced, remaining airborne for 460 ft before bouncing once again. After the second contact the pilot lowered the nose and streamed the braking parachute, assuming that he was on the runway, but in fact he was still 15–20 ft in the air. The aircraft struck the runway in a nose-down attitude, ripping off the nosewheel and bursting both main tyres. The port wheel assembly then broke away, after which the aircraft slid off the runway, shedding the starboard undercarriage leg before it came to rest. The pilot suffered spinal injuries as a result of the force of impact, which was later calculated at +10 g.

Landings with a strong crosswind component could also lead to difficulties. The maximum crosswind allowed by the RAF was 25 kts when landing on a dry runway, but at Warton, BAC test pilots were allowed to land with a crosswind of up to 30 kts when engaged in experimental flying. (Up to 1967, however, only eight landings had been made in a crosswind of 25 kts or above.) On 7 March 1967 BAC Chief Test Pilot Jimmy Dell, and co-pilot Peter Williams of Airwork, returned to Warton having carried out a general handling exercise in Lightning T.55 55-710. In their absence the wind had freshened considerably, and during the last of three approaches and overshoots to Runway 26 it was recorded at 180 degrees at 30 kts, gusting to 35 kts. A full stop landing was to follow the next approach, and the drift caused by the crosswind was counteracted with rudder, which Dell removed shortly before touchdown at 160–165 kts, just past the threshold markers. The nosewheel was lowered immediately and the braking parachute streamed.

At an early point in the landing run the aircraft assumed a right-wing-down attitude that was greater than had been noted on previous occasions. As the aircraft began to crab to starboard Dell applied full port braking, and the control column was moved progressively to port. Although the Lightning was pointing around 5 degrees port of the runway heading, it continued to slide to the right. The brake chute was jettisoned but it was obvious that the aircraft was going to drift off the runway. It was equally obvious that it was too late for a 'go-around' to be initiated. As forward speed reduced, the 'drift' angle appeared to increase. The aircraft left the runway still travelling at around 100 kts, and as the starboard wheel ran onto the grass it swerved violently to the right before hitting part of the arrester wire installation. An equally violent swerve to port followed as the port wing dug into the ground, during which the nose section broke, depositing Peter Williams, still in his seat, several feet away. The aircraft came to rest in a starboard-wing-down attitude, pointing south approximately 90 degrees to the runway. Both Dell and Williams suffered leg injuries.

FUEL STARVATION

Fuel monitoring had to be one of the Lightning pilot's highest priorities at all times, but occasionally it transpired that there was less available than there should have been. On 29 September 1965 Flt Lt Hedley Molland of 111 Squadron was returning to Wattisham in Lightning F.3

XP739, having carried out simulated attacks on a Canberra at 45,000 ft. At the beginning of his descent fuel was 1,200/1,200 lb, and on passing through 3,000 ft power was increased to 80 per cent on both engines. At this point the Fuel 1 low-pressure warning light appeared, followed by the corresponding Fuel 2 light. No. 1 engine rpm began to drop, and it then flamed out, the same sequence occurring on the No. 2 engine about ten seconds later. The relight buttons were pressed without success despite a fuel state at the time of 900/900 lb. After the failure to relight, Molland ejected at 1,500 ft and 250 kts, his aircraft gliding for another three miles before hitting the ground. As there had been ample fuel on board at the time of the crash, fuel starvation was the obvious cause of the accident, most probably owing to failure of the DC fuel transfer pumps, which had not supplied fuel to the collector tank for the fueldraulic booster pumps.

FOREIGN OBJECT DAMAGE

Although the ingestion of debris into the engines in flight was relatively rare, it did occur on two occasions. On 2 January 1967 Sqn Ldr Terry Carlton of 226 OCU, together with his student, Flt Lt Tony Gross, took off from Coltishall for a radar conversion exercise in Lightning T.4 XM971. During the climb out at about 10,000 ft there was a sharp explosion from the nose of the aircraft. At first it was thought that the nosewheel had burst, as shimmy had been reported on a previous flight, but after descending to circuit height throttle movement produced only a small increase in rpm, with an excessively high figure for JPT on both engines. It proved to be impossible to maintain height, and both pilots ejected about 2½ miles east of Coltishall. It was discovered that the accident was caused by over-pressurization of the radar bullet, and the subsequent detachment of the radome through overstressing, leading to debris from the radar scanner entering the engines.

Of the seventy-four Lightnings to be lost by the RAF, the circumstances surrounding the demise of F.6 XR763 were probably the most bizarre. During 5 Squadron's last Armament Practice Camp at RAF Akrotiri, Flt Lt Charlie Chan was detailed to carry out a live gunnery sortie against a towed target banner on 1 July 1987. On breaking away after his third pass Chan saw an object detach from the banner and was unable to avoid it hitting his aircraft. The rpm on No. 1 engine immediately fell to zero and JPT rose above 900° C, requiring that the engine be shut down. During an emergency approach into Akrotiri, JPT on No. 2 engine rose above limits and the pilot noticed a marked loss in thrust, to the extent that he had to apply full power in an attempt to maintain speed and height. This made little difference, however, and realizing that he would not be able to reach the runway, Chan turned to the right to avoid Akrotiri village and ejected safely at 250 ft and 150 kts. Examination of the target banner revealed that a round of ammunition had hit the upper wheel mounting, shattering it, and releasing the wheel into the air to be ingested by the No. 1 engine. This engine then seized, debris being ingested by the No. 2 in turn.

CHAPTER THIRTEEN

Pilot Debrief – 1

At the time of the Lightning's introduction into service, only experienced pilots with a minimum of one fighter tour behind them were allowed to get their hands on one. Having flown night-fighters for many years, including a spell as OC 89 Squadron on Venom NF.3s, Wg Cdr David Simmons AFC was well qualified to help introduce the Lightning into the RAF as the new boss of AFDS:

> My memories of the Lightning are mostly the lengthy preparation – avoiding the temptation to have a coffee beforehand, having a good pee, stripping down to shirt and long-johns, climbing into all the kit – g-suit, pressure jerkin, etc., carrying out your bone dome, climbing into the cockpit with difficulty and making all the connections inside. For me the flight was entirely ground radar controlled – climb to 36,000 ft, turn onto heading, accelerate to Mach 1.6 when cleared and then trade speed for height until the indicated airspeed fell towards the stall. During my time on Lightnings I never had to get my head into an AI. 23 visor when it could be easy to stray from the optimum flight path. There were no targets (at the time) on which to get Firestreak acquisition; we were just trying to determine timing, angle of climb, distance from start of acceleration, etc. At least I could concentrate on the flight instruments. In the very early days with the Lightning I recall getting to 62,000 ft but I would take my hat off to anyone who achieved acquisition on a U-2 at that height! It was certainly a bit lonely up there and there was very little room for error, though you felt secure in your pressurized cockpit, even if control was a bit sloppy.

With a tradition of aerobatics going back to its formative years, the RAF was keen to assess the Lightning for both solo and formation display flying, and it quickly became apparent that it was capable of carrying out manoeuvres that no other aircraft could perform, owing to its excess of power. One of the best exponents of the art of Lightning solo aero-batics was Sqn Ldr (later Air Cdre) Ken Goodwin, who was already a highly experienced Hunter display pilot:

My aerobatic life started on 92 Squadron (Meteor F.4s). The boss had seen me roll on take-off – retract the undercarriage when inverted – push until out of airspeed, then pull. I disappeared from sight in the Ouse valley and emerged a very shaken sprog pilot (300 hrs on jets!). Enquiries of my boss revealed he had never tried this routine. Suffice to say – from that time onwards I checked out routines at a safe height first. I suppose my busy time was from 1953 to 1957 in Germany on Hunter F.4s and F.6s with displays at Helsinki, Stockholm, Charleville, Avignon, Nurnberg, Amsterdam, Orange, etc. My routine consisted of a roll on take-off, slow-speed half-loop (250 kts), figure-of-8 with Derry turn, inverted flight, 8-point roll, Cuban-8 and an inverted break with negative 'g' to downwind for landing. The whole routine lasted 7½ to 8 minutes.

At CFE when the DB (Development Batch) Lightning was intro-duced it was soon evident to me that, in a way, this aircraft offered a much wider range of aerobatic manoeuvres through its amazing power to weight ratio which could reach nearly 1:1. I had seen Roly Beamont at Farnborough and soon discovered that 'square turns' were a more effective and rapid way of changing direction than the 400 kts, 4 g purist method advocated by CFS.

I was loaned to 74 Squadron with their Mk.1s for the duration of the Paris Air Show in 1961. With Squadron Leader John Howe leading, the show started with a diamond nine with me at the back. We were all relatively inexperienced, and from my vantage point it was astonishing to watch the tailplanes working overtime during low-speed manoeuvres to apparently little effect. We had to make a positive effort to stop 'stick stirring' or suffer a run of u/s tailplane motors! After two wing-overs as a nine, five of us departed to leave John with a four to conduct more complex formation manoeuvres. In between these it was my job to 'fill in' with Derry turns, loops, rolls, a figure-of-8 and a lot of afterburner. Le Bourget sits in a densely populated area and I can distinctly remember looking up to the tops of blocks of flats and the occupants waving!

I have already mentioned 'square turns'. It was not difficult to induce a high-speed stall below around 300 kts and it was remark-able how quickly one could wash off the speed with a concurrent deep buffet down to as low as 200 kts, even with the reheat engaged. Recovery was easily effected by releasing the stick back pressure – unstalling – then the remarkable acceleration of 10 kts per second per second. Unlike the Hunter with its ultra-light ailerons and heavy tailplane, the Lightning's controls were nicely balanced. For obvious reasons the rudder was not designed to have much authority so, for a really slow roll, it was a bit short in the final stages of this manoeuvre (also 8-point rolls) and at less than 300 kts one could not really keep the nose on the horizon. Certainly from a spectator's point of view, the 'square' turn at 250 kts with the burners ignited was quite spectacular, if not a bit hard on the ears! Generally, displays with the Lightning followed much the same routine as for the Hunter, while extenuating the special qualities of the Lightning including the spectacular rotation take-off which included a 220 kt 60-degree climb into a wing-over.

There have been display accidents, and whereas it was claimed the Lightning would not pitch up because of its 'notched delta' configuration, I thought otherwise, and gave evidence to this effect to a Board of Inquiry into a fatal display accident. At a practice display at Wattisham I was delayed for take-off and, unbeknown to me, I was using main tank (wing) fuel without a transfer from the ventral tank. A rotation take-off left me with an aft CG and a continuing pitch-up with the control column fully forward. I was able to use rudder and gentle aileron to get a wing-over going and the nose coming down laterally. I am quite certain we lost two pilots and aircraft through uncontrolled pitch up. Sadly, the Board of Inquiry was highly sceptical of my evidence.

Wg Cdr Martin Bee was another to excel at solo aerobatics in the Lightning, having also been a member of 74 Squadron's formation aerobatic team. He recalls his impressions of the Lightning and describes a typical solo routine:

The Lightning is a wonderful display aircraft. It has a powerful look, a huge slab-sided fuselage with polished 60-degree swept wings spearheaded by a radar cone. Below the nose cone is a stainless-steel airspeed probe way out in front. It exudes performance. A full load of fuel can be burned in about twelve minutes doing low level aerobatics. A good display without repetitions lasts about five minutes, leaving the watcher hoping for more. Thus a fuel load of full internals and an empty ventral tank is an ideal take-off weight and provides a thrust to weight ratio of a little more than 1:1 in full afterburner. Aerodynamic handling of the Lightning (unlike many US Century-series fighters) is impeccable. The aircraft can be pulled hard into a tight turn and the stick then relaxed slightly to hold a steady 5–6 g at around 400 knots. Pull a bit more, and the aircraft does not flick. It starts to mush as the angle of attack increases and the speed starts to fall off. Light the burners in a tight circuit at 200 knots with the gear and flaps down and keep the pull on to hold the speed at 200 knots. The Lightning turns on a sixpence with minimum roll off. Relax the back pressure and power must be immediately reduced to avoid rapid acceleration beyond gear and flap limits.

A solo aerobatic routine goes something like this. Line up on the runway, brakes fully on, increase power to no more than 80 per cent cold power to avoid sliding the aircraft on locked tyres. Release the brakes, push the throttles to 100 per cent and rock them outboard to the full afterburner detent. Two quick thumps are felt in the rear as the burners light and the aircraft accelerates to about 170 knots in seven seconds. Lift off gently, hold the aircraft a few feet above the runway and retract the gear. As speed reaches 200 knots (brave pilot), or 250 knots (not so brave), pull the stick back quickly and firmly to 'mush' the aircraft into a 70-degree climb. This is the famous 'rotation take-off' where a 4 g pull for milliseconds rotates the aircraft nose up without wing rock, while induced drag wipes the speed back to 170 knots again for the climb.

Then into the routine . . . fair weather . . . loops at 4–5 g, rolls and barrel rolls, lots of wing-overs to connect manoeuvres, tight 360s and a final high-speed run. Care has to be taken on the high-speed run not to break the sound barrier and cause heavy window and structural damage to buildings. Afterburner can be used initially to accelerate, but as 600 knots IAS is approached, both afterburners must be disengaged and cold power throttled back a few per cent so as not to exceed the local speed of sound (typically around 620–630 knots IAS at sea level). A bad-weather routine is much the same minus the loops, but with moist air the flat show has the advantage of being able to produce wonderful vortices from the wings and visible shock waves on the canopy. The circuit can be tight and showy, or quietly straight in while another display is in progress. Either way, finals is flown at 170 knots and the threshold crossed with power on at 165 knots. On touchdown the nose is lowered, throttles retarded and the drag chute is always streamed. Brakes are hardly used. The chute is jettisoned and the aircraft taxied back to the hangar with the pilot hoping that he has not overstressed it through sheer exuberance. The Lightning is a really great performer and a superb display aircraft.

Although he was a member of AFDS from 1959 to 1961, when the first Lightnings were being introduced to service, Sqn Ldr Wally Hill had to wait several more years before he finally got the chance to fly one:

It was policy to convert the ex-Hunter day-fighter pilots first, and much to my chagrin I was posted off to a ground tour before my name got to the head of the queue! It was not until January 1967 that I had the pleasure of converting to the Lightning as a Flight Commander of the newly formed 11 Squadron equipped with brand-new F.6 aircraft. Compared to the Javelin FAW.9 of 60 Squadron, which I had just left, the Lightning was, as expected, a revelation. The power and manoeuvrability was an eye-opener and to me it became simply the best aircraft I had flown. I like to call it the finest of the 'do it yourself' aircraft which you flew by feel without the intervention of any 'computery'. As a weapons system it was limited by the AI radar and its shortage of weapons and fuel, but for the task it was designed for it was more than adequate.

During my time on Lightnings I had no major incidents of any note. Number 11 Squadron were fortunate to be called upon to carry out Exercise Piscator – the practice reinforcement of Far East Air Force (FEAF) – during my tour. This involved flying ten aircraft to Singapore via Muharraq and Gan to Tengah and the recovery of nine aircraft (one was left with 74 Squadron) via Gan, Muharraq, Akrotiri to Leuchars. As a precursor to Piscator the squadron was required to do some endurance sorties to confirm that there was sufficient liquid oxygen (LOX) and fluids (hydraulics, lubricants, etc.) to safely fly from Leuchars to Muharraq (around 4,000 nm) and that pilot fatigue, in the cramped cockpit space and with a heavy workload, was not a problem. On 29 November 1967 Flt Lt Dave Eggleton flew an 8 hrs 15 min sortie and on 7 December the late Wg Cdr David Blucke (the Boss) and myself flew a pairs sortie of 8 hrs 25 min with five refuellings (close to 4,000 nm) together with practice interceptions just to tire us! On Piscator my trip Leuchars to Muharraq with Flg Off Brian Fuller as my No. 2 took the same 8 hrs 25 min.

On the return leg a Victor tanker blocked the runway at

Muharraq and my No. 2, Flt Lt Terry Butcher, and myself diverted to Sharjah since we were low on fuel and there was no estimate for clearing the Victor off the runway. At Sharjah we found, to our dismay, that there were no qualified brake chute packers, and since it would have totally upset the whole recovery process going on ahead of us (we were the last pair) to fly a packer from Muharraq back to Sharjah and then recover him, we did it ourselves. The Station Commander at Sharjah (an ex-Javelin navigator whom I knew) had an empty hangar swept clean of sand and any contamination. Terry and I then spread the parachutes out and discussed and argued about how they should be packed. We cobbled the two chutes together, fitted them to our aircraft, sweated gallons of liquid in the process and guess what, they worked!

Having spent all his RAF flying career on night and all-weather fighters (Meteor NF, Javelin and Lightning), Wally Hill's final posting was as OC Operations Wing at Binbrook from 1982 to 1985.

Following his conversion to the Lightning at Middleton St George in 1963, Flt Lt Peter Vangucci flew F.1s and F.3s with 74 Squadron:

74(F) Squadron had been the first to re-equip with the Lightning and was still flying the original F.1. We flew a typical mixture of sorties for an all-weather, air defence fighter squadron: practice interceptions, snake climbs, formation, tail chases (combat was not officially allowed), aerobatics and some navigation, although the latter was high on the agenda for every sortie as the F.1 was always short of fuel and you always had to think about your recovery. Night flying, practice diversions, squadron detachments and Fighter Command exercises also played their normal part.

The aircraft was big and could be a bit of a handful for the last 200 feet of the approach and landing. But it was an absolute joy to fly; it was a pilot's aircraft. If you wanted to do something – fly fast, slow, high, low or just go straight up – you could do it. Indeed, one of the only bad moments associated with the aircraft was climbing out of the cockpit when you were diverted to an airfield which had no Lightning cockpit ladders. It was a long way down to the ground and too easy to fall!

Two other comments spring to mind. The first concerned fuel, which was always in short supply, even leading to the need (if the weather was really bad) to prepare for recovery almost as soon as you were airborne. I can remember on a number of occasions when the weather was bad in East Anglia and the diversions were a long way away, that I only had enough fuel for take-off, climb to 36,000 ft, transit to the dive circle and immediately start my descent to land. Not good for building up the hours! The other was a tendency to induce vertigo in the pilot, especially during steep turns on a pitch-black night. You simply had to ignore your senses and believe your instruments and nothing else.

In February 1964 the squadron moved to Leuchars, and in June of that year we re-equipped with the new Lightning F.3. This mark had updated radar, a better autopilot and the OR946 instrumentation, which was a mixture of digital and analogue instruments and almost wholly electrically driven. The F.3, with the extra-large fin and rudder, was the first to be cleared to Mach 2.0, and everyone enjoyed flying at this milestone speed which was reached after climbing to around 40,000 ft. If anything the F.3 was even more short of fuel than the earlier marks.

When we flew into Leuchars the station had enjoyed the reputation of having one of the best weather factors in Britain. We soon found out why. All previous aircraft stationed there had been able to land downwind from the sea towards the west if the tailwind component was not too high. The Lightning could take no downwind component. In a light wind off the sea, the haar (a kind of moving or lifted fog) would drift over the airfield. At night this was practically invisible from the ground and was no trouble if you were landing from the sea. However, it piled up against a small hill just a few hundred yards inland from the circuit on the easterly runway. So we would return intending to carry out a night visual circuit. At the end of the downwind leg the turn-in would start with the runway clearly in sight. Suddenly, half-way round you popped into unannounced cloud (the haar). The runway lights went out, one was very conscious of the hill which was just under one's feet in the banked turn, there was no instrument approach available and time was of the essence due to fuel, or rather lack of it, again. We soon found that the Lightning's greater demands made the Leuchars weather factor drop to a much lower level, to the detriment of our flying hours.

Although many pilots were to complete a tour on Lightnings without having to contend with a major systems malfunction, such situations were guaranteed to occur during a trip in the simulator, especially if engaged on a 'saturation' sortie, which covered almost every possible emergency in one session. Initially many of the warnings would be cancelled once the pilot had dealt with them correctly, but eventually the various emergencies would remain, requiring the pilot to take whatever action was necessary, including the correct R/T calls, before recovering to base or diverting. The sortie usually involved a practice interception, the unfortunate pilot having to contend with anything from subsonic targets at varying heights, to supersonic head-on attacks, the emergencies usually being introduced when he was deep into an attack and concentrating on achieving a 'kill'.

During any Lightning interception, real or simulated, the amount of time available was very short. Assuming a radar pick-up range of 28 miles and a collision course heading, with a subsonic target, closure time to impact was around 90 seconds. However, if the threat was supersonic, this figure was reduced to less than 50 seconds. In that time the pilot had to take the appropriate action so that a successful interception could be achieved. Since any manoeuvring had to be started well before the potential collision time, together with various arming procedures, fuel and position checks, there was very little time available and the pressure was intense. Wg Cdr Brian Carroll describes a typical 'saturation' sortie, one that he had to perform prior to taking responsibility for the simulator section at Leuchars:

> With the briefing over I climb into the cockpit, checking carefully that all is correct (the staff have a nasty habit of rerigging the ejection seat, setting the U/C lever in the UP position, the trigger in the 'commit' position – anything missed is a black mark). Seventeen checks cover the ejector seat plus essential checks in the cockpit, like ensuring that the U/C lever is in the DOWN position, the master armament switch is OFF, guns/missile trigger on SAFE, etc., before sitting in. Then there are thirty-four pre-strap-in checks, and if all is well, strap in, adjust rudder pedals, remove and stow the seat pins. Now for the rest of the checks before starting engines, only eighty-two of them, and many of these will have been rigged, either prior to getting into the cockpit or by being switched to a failed indication after checking. Finally it is time to start the engines and still more checks, but only four of them (it's getting easier).
>
>   Switches on, external power on line, start No. 1 – rpm looking OK, all associated warning lights out at the correct time and everything looks good. Press No. 2 – warning lights out, but the Jet Pipe Temperature is climbing fast (800° C max and 750° C at idle) and is obviously going to exceed limits, so HP cock off to close the engine down. The fault is now removed so I start No. 2 engine

again. This part of the trip takes some time as various snags are introduced, i.e. engine fires . . . oil warning lights . . . hydraulic warnings (either flying controls or the services system) . . ., but eventually all is well and after start checks (twenty-five of them) it is time to call for taxi clearance.

After carrying out the take-off checks, various malfunctions are again engineered and as it is a night sortie, with only the dull glow of cockpit lighting available, it is all too easy to miss something. Take-off flap is selected (F.6), but the indicator only goes part-way down, a fuel warning light flickers on and off very briefly, so I keep a 'third' eye on the panel in case it flickers again. By now the voltage is slightly low, services pressure is slowly falling towards 2,000 psi (it should be 3,000 psi ±250) and the oxygen contents, which was OK to start with, has suddenly fallen close to zero (this gauge is not exactly 'in scan', being low down and underneath one's right elbow). All these problems would normally mean an abort, of course, but they are all cured once spotted and the correct action taken. At last the flight is finally cleared for take-off.

Lined up and ready to roll, I carry out a really close check around the cockpit; rpm is slowly increased to 92 per cent, brakes holding OK, a final look around and it's full cold power, a slight pause, and into full reheat as the aircraft accelerates as only a Lightning can. The nosewheel is raised and a few seconds later I am airborne, U/C selected up (it has to be fully retracted by 250 kts, otherwise air pressure will not allow full lock-up), but a starboard red remains on. I pull back on the power, level off (keeping below the limit of 250 kts) while looking for a possible reason. It transpires that the services pressure has fallen to zero. I carry out the vital action, inform ATC of my intentions, select down to see what I get, two reds and nothing on the nosewheel. I inform ATC of the new situation and advise that I wish to join the ILS for an emergency approach to land. Flaps are selected down but no movement is indicated – I may get them when the Emergency U/C is selected, this is done at 200 kts maximum. I will have no airbrakes, and the wheel brakes will only have accumulator pressure so gentle braking will be needed, followed by a tow from the runway. However, I then get an OK from outside, all the problems are removed and I am cleared to continue the climb-out to FL 350. I am instructed to call radar on Stud 7. The remainder of the climb-out is uneventful and I level off at FL 350 under radar control and ready for a few interceptions.

Southern Radar – 'Red 1 (my call sign) we have a hostile target in your one o'clock, range 50, height and speed unknown, maintain your present heading and advise contact.'

Red 1 – 'Roger, maintaining height and heading.'

I now busily search for the target (it can be at any height, speed and heading). I finally get a weak response and work out that it is some 15,000 ft below me and looks to be just supersonic. I lay off some 20 degrees to starboard and when in position start a descending turn at full cold power, aiming to roll in behind the target at around two miles. My height advantage will give me most of the acceleration needed to effect a good closing speed, and only when approaching the stern position will I engage reheat if this is needed (fuel conservation always being uppermost in one's thoughts). Weapons are checked and armed, switches made safe, but I stay in intermittent search mode since a lock-on would alert the intruder of my presence. I call radar for clearance to fire. Permission is given, the radar locks on, missiles acquire, in range, missile released, target killed.

Red 1 – 'Target "splashed". Climbing back to FL 350.'

Southern Radar – 'Negative Red 1, we have another target for you, estimated low level, probable height is 500 ft, come left onto 060 and descend to 3,000 ft. Target is range 45, when on heading it will be in your 12 o'clock.'

Red 1 – 'Roger.'

Red 1 – 'Steady on 060, passing FL 150 request QNH.'

Southern Control – 'Red 1 the QNH is 1023.'

Red 1 – 'Roger Radar 1023 now set, levelling at 3,000 ft, I have a contact crossing at 12 miles.'

Southern Radar – 'Red 1 that is your target, you are cleared to close and identify only.'

Red 1 – 'Roger Radar, closing to identify.'

This means getting in close using the radar's Vis Ident facility and closing to 300 yards or less (of course in the simulator there is nothing to see, but they who are giving me a hard time simply want to observe the correct procedure).

Red 1 – 'Southern Radar, the target is a Canberra at 300 ft heading 015 degrees at 330 kts, breaking off and climbing.'

Southern Radar – 'Red 1 we have another target at high level, range 130 miles, state your fuel.'

Red 1 – 'Insufficient remaining, am returning to base (I am now given several thousand pounds of fuel, thus allowing the torture to continue!). Affirmative Radar, fuel state is Bingo 2, climbing to FL 350, request vector.'

Southern Radar – 'Red 1 vector 178 degrees Buster, Buster, advise at FL 350.'

Red 1 – 'Southern Radar Red 1 now at FL 350.'

Southern Radar – 'Roger Red 1, your target is 12 o'clock, range 65, estimated altitude FL 600.'

Red 1 – 'Going high speed, keep me advised.'

Southern Radar – 'Target range now 30 dead ahead.'

Red 1 – 'Starting climb (my speed is now 1.5 Mach), contact, "Judy".'

Then all hell breaks loose. Noise in the cockpit, the Fire 1 caption illuminates and JPT is going off the clock. I cancel both reheats and bring both engines back to idle/idle (normally one of the engines needs to be at fast idle to keep the AC power on line, but at high altitude idle rpm is high enough). No. 1 engine is closed down, both high- and low-pressure fuel to OFF along with the DC pumps. Making a hard turn (to reduce speed to around 250 kts) towards base I make a Mayday call on 243. Speed has now decayed and the fire extinguisher button is pressed to see whether the fire will go out. Meanwhile I am in a cruise descent at 250 kts, a speed that I will maintain during recovery. Should the fire not go out I will be in a bale-out situation. Radar clear me to recover to base, advising that the weather has deteriorated and is bordering on RED which would entail diverting should it actually go RED (thanks guys!) Other considerations with No. 1 engine out of commission are several, U/C Emergency system will be inoperative unless idle rpm is above 30 per cent and there will probably be no brake chute.

I continue monitoring all the cockpit indications. Five minutes have gone and the fire warning is still on, now approaching FL 200 and I have increased power on No. 2 to keep the AC electrics on line and to give a little more cockpit heat, thus preventing any misting up when I am eventually on final approach. The fuel situation is reasonable; however, I have to consider the possibility of needing to transfer fuel from the No. 1 side to the live engine; the transfer rate will be slow, so I need to give it plenty of time to be effective. The weather has become much worse, heavy rain, medium to severe turbulence, lightning flashes that illuminate the cockpit, and a cloud base of 500 ft with visibility of 2,000 yards. Not looking too good, but sufficient to get in. Coltishall Approach now comes in on the act.

Coltishall – 'Red 1 how do you read?'

Red 1 – 'Loud and clear Coltishall.' (I nearly say left to right, but fight the temptation!)

Coltishall – 'Reading you 5s also, what is your condition?'

Red 1 – 'The fire caption has gone out, otherwise all is . . . standby Coltishall, my main instruments have just failed (standby horizon, compass, altimeter and ASI look OK), am continuing with this approach, range now 23 miles and level 5,000 ft. Confirm QNH and present weather.'

Coltishall – 'Red 1 QNH is now 1010, we have a severe thunderstorm 3 miles from the field, the wind has now moved across the runway, giving a crosswind component of 15 gusting to 25 kts, you are now No. 2 in pattern, one ahead has low fuel and intends to land. What is your fuel state?'

Red 1 – 'I have 1,400 lb on the live engine and 700 remaining on the dead engine.'

Coltishall – 'Roger clear to continue, advise ILS contact, our main radar has just failed.'

Coltishall – 'Red 1, this is Coltishall, the aircraft ahead of you has engaged the crash barrier, you are to divert to Wattisham.' (I start fuel transfer from No. 1 engine to No. 2.)

Red 1 – 'Thank you Coltishall, turning left and maintaining 5,000 ft, advise Wattisham that I will be on less than minimum fuel and request priority to land.'

With some 60 miles to go my fuel state is critical, my fuel burn for the 60 miles will be around 900 lb (at best) leaving me with less than minimum, so I have no option but to cross-feed the fuel. With the aircraft still clean I set off for Wattisham, still battling with turbulence, lightning and other radio interference. I now notice that I am using higher rpm than usual to maintain speed and so suspect that the standby ASI is playing up, probably due to icing. I switch to an alternative power supply (this cures the problem). I also decide that it is time to get my own back on the sadistic guys outside who are undoubtedly enjoying themselves no end while I am sweating and struggling to keep the beast in the air.

I decide to go 'speechless'. This means that I have now simulated a microphone failure and can only communicate by means of Morse code. This, I am delighted to say, throws the examiners into considerable confusion, so much so that they forget to generate any more emergencies and I recover successfully to Wattisham without further assistance. I emerge from the simulator a mere shadow of my former self, and on opening the hood I am greeted by cries of 'foul' by the examiner, one Vaughan Radford, who assures me that it was his intention to force a bale-out and/or a crash. All in all, the score is probably one to the examiners and one to me!

Having finished his tour with 74 Squadron in December 1964, Peter Vangucci was then posted to 226 OCU (by now at Coltishall) as OC 1 Squadron:

We flew the T.4 for dual instruction and the F.1A for solo work. Here again, apart from the sheer pleasure of the job and the aircraft, two thoughts seem worth comment. Hitherto all Lightning pilots had been converted from other fighter aircraft – usually the Hunter, but sometimes the Javelin. Now first-tour pilots, that is young students who had just completed their flying training, had begun flying the Lightning. They were first-class material and some rose to the highest ranks in the Service. Initially all went well but after a time we noticed a slight disappointment and lack of enthusiasm among the students arriving at the OCU. It transpired that they had been led to believe that the Lightning was so big and heavy it could not compare with, say, the Hunter for manoeuvrability and pleasure of flying. Clearly something needed to be done.

We initiated a flying programme for Day One of each new course, before the students went to ground school and the simulator. It was meant as a taster for what was to come. The instructor did all the flying (we had to have some perks!) and the student just sat back and watched. The sortie started with a reheat take-off and climb to 36,000 ft which took about 90 seconds. We then accelerated to Mach 1.3 – they'd never been supersonic straight and level before – and pulled some very steep turns to show the excellent supersonic handling. Then a maximum rate of descent to 2,000 ft, followed by a deceleration to 250 knots and some demonstration handling at slow speed. Next we lit both reheats and sat back to see the reaction. At about Mach 0.94 we went into an absolutely vertical climb. At about 25,000 ft still going straight up we finally cancelled reheat, pulled over the top, returned to base and landed. There was no more talk of the unmanoeuvrable or clumsy Lightning!

The other problem area for the first tourist was the question of pilot height and, more specifically, leg length. This arose because in the early days selection of the first Lightning pilots had been restricted to those under 5 ft 6 in, the so-called 'league of little men'. The RAF soon ran out of pilots that size and took anyone, which was just as well for me as I am over 6 ft tall. But the myth remained that on ejection tall pilots would lose at least their knee caps and maybe more of their legs on the cockpit coaming. Reassurance from people as tall as me was not really the answer as they knew we would have done anything to remain on Lightnings. So I arranged for a team to stand by in the hangar with a seat in a Lightning being serviced attached to a Coles crane. At the first night's beer call, as soon as the conversation turned to ejections (and knees) all those students who were interested or worried were dispatched to the hangar, where 'Chiefy' strapped them in, hauled them up, showed them all was well, patted them on the head and sent them back to relax again at the beer call. It sounds very simple and it was, but it worked. In my two years at the OCU we never had anyone fail to clear the coaming.

During the Cold War one of the principal duties of the Lightning force was Quick Reaction Alert (QRA), whereby aircraft would be scrambled to intercept and identify any unidentified aircraft entering UK airspace. Owing to its northerly location, Leuchars bore the brunt of QRA activity as Tu-95 *Bears* regularly flew from their bases in northern Russia to test the UK's air defences. Brian Carroll describes a QRA with a difference that he flew in October 1968:

Holding QRA was always something of an unknown quantity. You could spend hours of inactivity being lulled into a false sense of security; then, when you least expected it, all hell broke loose and the game was on. Night QRA was often very restful, a couple of good books to read (and the ever welcome cups of tea) could be the most excitement that one would get, but on the other hand it could be quite hectic.

The first action on taking over alert duties was to look around the aircraft, an external check to see that all was well (our ground crew could always be relied upon to ensure that there were no problems in that area), ejection seat live, essential switches set to ON and straps adjusted. We could then retire to our rest room and await any action that might come our way. Being based at Leuchars we always anticipated a northerly scramble heading. The Russian *Bears* were our bread and butter, always sneaking down from the Iceland/Faeroes gap, so when a different vector was given it really was quite a surprise.

Two of us had settled down for the night and were enjoying a little shut-eye when the scramble was called at 0220 hrs, when one is probably not as sharp as normal. We were quickly into our respective aircraft and talking to GCI at Boulmer on the landline. Initially we were on a 10-minute state that gave us plenty of time to get a full briefing on the weather, the state of our diversion airfields and the possible threat that had brought us out of our slumber. After a short wait we were informed that only one aircraft was required to go and I was in the 'hot seat'. My number two climbed down and returned to the rest room just as I was given the order to scramble. All switches on, a clearance wave from the ground crew and both engines were soon running.

Moving out of the 'Q' shed, I was now in radio contact with the tower, who automatically gave me the runway in use, QFE, wind direction and clearance for take-off. The night was really dark with no moon and a scattering of thin cirrus cloud that hid most of the stars. It was going to be difficult to see very much in these conditions. Otherwise the weather was fine, so the recovery

should not present any problems. The first surprise was the intercept vector, as I was told to make FL 350 and head 090 degrees,
subsonic cruise. Four minutes later I was settled at height and
easing along at a little over 0.9 Mach. It really was very dark, there
was nothing to see at all either visually or on the radar. The
outside air temperature was a cool –56° C, but thanks to excellent
conditioning, the cockpit was pleasantly warm.

I was held on this easterly heading for quite a while and began
to wonder just where I was going to end up, as the Dutch coast
was looming ever closer. All this time I had little to do other than
check that all the systems were OK, that there was plenty of fuel
and also to keep a weather eye on the radar. Otherwise I could
relax. Boulmer finally came to life again, informing me that there
was an unknown target at range 30, heading northerly. My
instructions were to turn port onto a NE heading and close
with the target. Shortly after this I made radar contact and
continued the chase, informing Boulmer that I was *Contact, and
Judy,* meaning that I did not need any further assistance. In time I
had closed to around 500 yards but could see nothing of my target.
I informed Boulmer of this fact, and that as the *unknown* was not
showing any lights there was little chance of making a positive
identification.

After a short break, Boulmer came back with instructions that a
positive ident was essential. With this I started to close in again.
Although my radar set was behaving really well and holding an
excellent lock, I could still see nothing as I closed to minimum
radar distance. I was now very close and slightly below the target,
having felt slight turbulence once or twice as my fin encountered
jet wash. At last I was able to make out a vague shape that was
marginally denser than the surrounding sky, but not enough to
tell what it was, other than it was fairly large, but then I already
knew that from my initial radar response. By now I was hoping
that whoever was flying this unknown aircraft would not make
any sudden changes of speed, height or direction as I was tucked
well in underneath him and would not be readily aware of any
such movement.

Trying to maintain station while looking nearly vertically
upwards through the canopy was putting quite a strain on my
neck. In addition, I also had to keep a weather eye on my range
from base and, more importantly, my fuel state. In all, I must have
held that position for 8–10 minutes. I was still little wiser as to
what type of aircraft it was. By now my fuel was the critical factor,
and calling Boulmer, I informed them that I needed to break off

and return to base. As to what the target was I would hazard a guess and call it a KC-135. This was obviously the magic phrase since all the lights in the world were switched on and there was my KC in all its glory. Boulmer also confirmed that this was correct, obviously having known full well what I was shadowing for what seemed, to me, like a week. It also came to my ears that the tanker crew were very well aware of my presence and had absolutely no intention of twitching so much as an eyebrow, knowing that a Lightning was tucked in right below them. I was never sure just how close I was, but there could not have been an excess of clearance between their belly and my fin. No doubt they were just as relieved as I was when I finally broke away for recovery.

My heading for base was now 210 degrees at 190 nm, which placed me abeam the northern point of the Orkneys, in good range of Lossiemouth should I need to divert. However, with the weather remaining fine, a recovery to Leuchars was going to be OK, taking 23 minutes at economic cruise with a free let-down for a visual straight-in approach and landing on Runway 27. The radar in the Lightning was quite good for navigation once you were used to it. At range, the ground returns were fairly easy to recognize (only becoming badly distorted when close up), so St Andrews bay and the Eden estuary were easily seen as I cruised homewards. It was even possible to lock the radar onto one of the hangars and that enabled one to track into the airfield in poor weather.

This particular night the runway lights were visible at around 70 miles, so, aiming at them, I started a fast let-down, increasing to 1.3 Mach, planning to be subsonic by the time I was 45 miles from the coast. After a 'goodnight' call to Boulmer, I changed to base frequency, obtained clearance to land and with 10 miles to go I was level at 1,500 ft and dawdling at 240 kts. Gear and flaps were selected for landing, speed brought back to 175 kts as the aircraft descended slowly towards touchdown at 160 kts. A precautionary landing, engines to idle/idle, wheel brakes applied and brake chute deployed, a sharp tug as the chute bit, wheel brakes off, chute dropped before turning off the runway, and a slow taxi back to the 'Q' shed where the ground crews were waiting to refuel and turn the aircraft round for another scramble, should there be one.

Back in the QRA rest room, my partner was still awake and keen to know what had been going on. As ever, there was endless paperwork to fill in and yet more tea. I had just finished writing when the phone rang. We were both on our feet ready for another scramble but it was just my controller wishing to chat about my sortie. He confirmed that they were all well aware of the target's identity, and that the KC's crew knew all about my close proximity and had no intentions of doing anything silly while I was close by. I did suggest that they could have offered me some fuel after all my efforts, but that would have cost Dollars. I am quite sure that neither the controller nor the KC captain realized just how difficult that sortie was, and perhaps that is just as well.

Pilot Debrief – 2

Although the dream of every RAF fast jet pilot was to be posted to a Lightning squadron, even if the dream came true it would not be too long before he became tour-expired (usually around 3–4 years) and he would be faced with a break from operational flying. Ground tours varied tremendously, one of the more interesting ones being a posting to the Central Tactics and Trials Organization (CTTO) located at High Wycombe, alongside RAF Strike Command HQ. Peter Vangucci found himself there in April 1968 with special responsibility for the Lightning:

I gained the impression when I started the job that a number of quite senior people thought there was little left to do with the Lightning and that other aircraft, either just in service or destined to enter service in the near future, were far more important. In reality there was much to do as a lot of very good advice had been ignored in the past and there had been a shortage of staff officers with front-line Lightning experience.

Any record of my work during this time would be out of balance if mention were not made of the first Officer Commanding CTTO, Air Cdre (later ACM Sir) David Evans. He quickly grasped that further development of the Lightning needed to be done, and needed to be done urgently or it would be too late. As a consequence, his support and his personal contribution were of enormous benefit. Although I spent over three years at CTTO and was involved for all that time in various Lightning projects, there were three major initiatives which could be mentioned as each one was a 'first' for the RAF, at least in modern times.

During a visit to Boscombe Down early in my tour I discovered that a trial was about to start to prove the Aden gun being fitted to the ventral tank of the Lightning Mark 6. The gun installation was being developed for the Saudi Arabians but would also be fitted to RAF aircraft once the system had been proved. A large amount of ammunition, around 100,000 rounds, was to be fired to show that the mounting was safe, and the Saudis were paying the costs of the whole trial. I discovered that the rounds were to be fired into the air over a wide performance envelope, but with no attempt made to measure the accuracy of the system or the gunsight.

I was horrified. This was a rerun of the unfortunate saga of the first gun trial on the original Mark 1 Lightning which had needed 74 Squadron to sort out the mess in 1962/3. I hurriedly saw David Evans on my return to High Wycombe, expressed my concern and suggested what should be done to correct what I saw as a major omission. At his behest I wrote a paper arguing that the RAF should always measure system accuracy when proving system installation and that the policy should start with the proposed Lightning trials scheduled to begin in the very near future. It was CTTO's first major initiative, and Air Cdre Evans drove the proposal through with great skill and even greater determination until it was accepted. The Air Force Board decreed that, from then on, Weapon System Accuracy Trials should always be combined with the armament safety trials of all future aircraft fitted with integral guns. The accuracy of the Lightning Mark 6 ventral-tank gun and gunsight was established before the gun was fitted to production aircraft for the Royal Saudi Air Force and for the RAF.

The second initiative arose from access I was afforded to some classified work on aircraft energy performance by the United States Air Force. I helped CTTO scientific staff develop a computer model which could give energy-manoeuvring graphs for the Lightning in practically all situations. From these I was able produce a Lightning Tactics Manual which gave information on all aspects of Lightning operations, including a classified section on comparative performance with other fighter aircraft on both sides of the Iron Curtain. Again Air Cdre Evans drove through the agreement for money to be made available to meet costs, and the project was established as the first in a line of future 'tactics' manuals.

The last initiative which warrants mention concerns the Lightning weapons instructors known as 'IWIs', the Interceptor Weapons Instructors. There were normally two on each squadron, together with a number at the OCU who taught the IWI course. The course was very high pressure and very detailed, and I knew that, once graduated, IWIs were a highly trained, highly skilled, extremely knowledgeable asset for a squadron. Since the courses had started, the Lightning had been deployed to Germany, Cyprus and Singapore, where the different environments called for the development of new tactics and the amendment of some old ones. Unfortunately, there were no means by which these advances could be shared between the different theatres and different squadrons. IWIs also honed their skills after returning to their squadrons on completion of the course, and it was difficult for them to share these experiences with other IWIs.

Once more I approached David Evans. He obtained funding for a conference of all the RAF's IWIs to be held at High Wycombe, and opened the first day's programme himself. The conference was a great success and the exchange of experiences, dissemination of ideas and development of future tactics was well worth the effort and costs involved. The annual IWI conference became an established feature of the Lightning force and ran for many years on other fighter aircraft.

The Interceptor Weapons Instructor had one of the most important tasks on an operational squadron as he was responsible for ensuring that all pilots were mission capable in terms of their ability to handle the Lightning as a weapon system in all tactical situations. Flt Lt Trevor MacDonald-Bennett took the IWI course at Coltishall in the middle of his first tour with 74 Squadron at Tengah:

I was fortunate to be selected for the IWI course and returned to the UK for three months during the winter of 1968. It was without doubt the most intensive course which I have ever encountered, and I felt that I had really earned the title of IWI at its conclusion! Each course comprised two students working with a team of three IWI staff instructors. My co-student was a pilot on 56 Squadron based in Cyprus, so I think we were able to pass on some interesting tactical advice from our own unique theatres of operation that was helpful for later courses. Weather and serviceability permitting, we would fly twice each day, normally in the morning or afternoon, with the remainder of the day involved with lectures, study, and preparation for the following day's flying programme. The flying was divided into specific phases such as subsonic, supersonic, ECM (electronic countermeasures), low level, ACM (air combat manoeuvring), etc.

Lectures were initially presented by staff instructors to demonstrate expected standards, with progressively more subjects given to the students for research and presentation. Subjects were mainly orientated around the weapons system (radar, missiles, Aden cannon), interception techniques including ground-based systems, capabilities of threat aircraft and systems, etc. Morning met briefings were normally presented by the students, along with the flying briefing, and later in the course they were expected to plan, present and brief a small exercise for the benefit of the whole station. Because of the very intensive nature of the course, we had priority on aircraft that, combined with a perceived rather élitist nature of the position, sometimes caused a little resentment among the 'regular' OCU staff. We also enjoyed the luxury of our own detached briefing area, which probably didn't help improve our image!

On completion of the course the newly qualified weapons instructor returned to his squadron, where the workload, if anything, was even greater than it had been during training.

On a day-to-day basis the task of the IWI covered routines such as planning and running regular training programmes to ensure that pilots remained current and effective in all our operational roles. He also flew regularly with all squadron members to ensure standardization and competence. Any new arrivals would initially be put under the IWI's wing to monitor his progress throughout a syllabus designed to bring him up to operational status. The organization and planning of any live missile firings would be part of the IWI's remit (and his fault if unsuccessful!). All squadron members were encouraged to consider new ideas and tactics, and should a trial of the same be undertaken, the IWI would normally be responsible for the planning, liaison with other squadrons involved, and so on. He was also expected to lecture on a regular basis on all things associated with our weapons system and tactics and stay in touch with our engineers and armourers to discuss any changes or modifications. Simulator instructors played a very important role in our training programme, and it could be very easy to unintentionally exclude them from current thinking and changes. This was another area of IWI involvement.

We were particularly lucky at Tengah with regular visitors from the Royal Navy, RAAF, RAF Vulcans and Victors, etc. These presented superb opportunities for mutual training and experience, but required very careful disciplined briefing to avoid things getting out of hand and impacting on flight safety. We also enjoyed superb detachments in Malaysia with the Australian Mirages and visits to Darwin in Northern Australia for 'flag flying' and exercises. Major exercises were the responsibility of HQ staff at Changi, but at a local level all squadron members became involved, with emphasis on weapons and tactics again falling on the IWI. One problem with one IWI per squadron was the two-Flight system where typically one Flight would be day-flying while the other operated at night. The case was therefore made for two IWIs per squadron, which greatly enhanced the position and lowered the workload. During my time the Lightning was operational in UK, Germany, Cyprus and Singapore. Each of these theatres demanded very different tactics and techniques. The local IWI was therefore very much encouraged to spread the word to ensure that the Lightning force was fully up to speed with current thinking and operations.

After leaving 74 Squadron my final tour was on the IWI staff at Coltishall, so I was very conscious of the 'them and us' atmosphere which I had detected as a student. I was pleased to discover that it was less obvious, and whenever possible we tried to fly with normal OCU students as well as IWI students. Students and staff alike were continually coming up with innovative ideas to improve systems, but it was clear that there was a resignation to the fact that there was no intention to make any worthwhile changes. One satisfying event was being part of a gun-firing trial conducted on T.4s and F.1As at St Mawgan to prove the viability of guns in the air-to-air role. They were, of course, later incorporated in the ventral tanks of the F.6 and I believe were used very successfully in regular training against airborne towed banners.

During the early stages of flying training most pilots experience the feeling that they are never going to be able to master all the various facets of flying an aircraft. To begin with basic control seems to require full concentration, and they find that they have no spare capacity for lookout, R/T, navigation, monitoring of instruments and all the other aspects of good piloting. Gradually things become easier, and the new pilot finds that he is able to perform several tasks simultaneously. Military pilots have an additional problem in that as soon as they master one particular machine they are required to move on to a more advanced type, usually with more complex systems and much greater performance. Even though a pilot may have been at home in a Hunter, his first flight in a Lightning could make him feel that he was right back at square one. In the early 1970s Brian Carroll was an instructor with 226 OCU at Coltishall. He recalls a night scramble with a newly arrived student:

In addition to our training commitments, converting pilots from the Hunter OCU and others returning from ground jobs, we were also tasked as a front-line squadron, carrying the crest of No. 65 Squadron. As such we were liable to be subjected to TACEVALS (a Tactical Evaluation Exercise called at zero notice and usually in the early hours when all were asleep). On one such occasion a new course of students had just arrived. They had completed their initial ground-school programme of lectures and were reasonably conversant with the Lightning's systems and operating procedures. They had also started Flight Simulator sorties and had been airborne on Exercise 1, the 'Instructor's Benefit' sortie during which the full potential of the aircraft was demonstrated. A TACEVAL was called one night in October 1971, and the weather was cold and wet with steady rain that had been falling all the previous day and was to continue for the next 48 hours. Cloud was extensive, the lowest being around 800–1,000 ft and going all the way to 30,000 ft without a break, just the sort of weather that fighter pilots dream about (well maybe on a bad day!).

Within a very short time the squadron was a hive of activity, the ground crews were working at a feverish pitch, pre-flight inspections were being completed as rapidly as possible, aircraft were then positioned in their predetermined slots, ready for the pilots to carry out their own pre-flight checks and set the cockpit ready for a fast getaway. Weather and exercise briefings for the aircrews were all well under way, emergency and other procedures were all covered and we then awaited the first call from the control centre to start the ball rolling. Meanwhile the new course of students was being kept busy with routine jobs in operations (and the coffee bar). As we operated a number of two-seaters (Lightning T.4s), it was decided that we would fly as many of the new course students as possible in the right-hand seat to let them see what operating the aircraft as a weapons system was all about. They had, of course, no knowledge at this time of the radar, so it was left to each instructor to attempt to brief on that aspect during the sortie, time permitting.

Word finally came through to bring a number of crews to cockpit readiness, I had been allocated a T.4 and so had a student with me. I had already carried out my pre-flight inspection so we were able to climb straight into the cockpit, strapping in took a few moments, we put our helmets on and our communications were now routed via the telebrief facility. Ground supplies, AC and DC were on line, radio frequency was selected, flight instruments erected, weapons checked, all ready to start engines as soon as scramble instructions were received. We had only been strapped in a few minutes when the controller said, 'Eagle 04 (my call sign) vector 120, make Flight Level 220, when airborne call on Stud 7, SCRAMBLE.'

Three minutes later we entered the active runway, applying full power and accelerating, the runway lights blurring as we raced into the darkness. Airborne, gear retracted, a hard turn onto our designated heading of 120 degrees, and into a standard climb as we changed frequency to Stud 7. Now snug and warm in what I called my 'airborne office' (it was nice to be out of the rain), I explained briefly what the radar picture was showing, though I doubt that my passenger was able to make much of the orange display. Less than two minutes had passed since we entered the runway when we levelled off at 22,000 ft. Our target was said to be at 25,000 ft some 40 miles away crossing our track from right to left, and to this day I do not think that my student actually saw the contact on the radar, even though I talked the attack right through to the 'kill'. We were, of course, in thick cloud so never made visual contact with the hostile intruder.

As I broke away from this interception new instructions were passed from ground radar to intercept another target, this one at high level and closing fast. Reheats were engaged and a rapid climb made to 36,000 ft. Speed was increased to Mach 1.3, weapons were rearmed and as we closed from astern I pulled the aircraft into a steep climb in an attempt to scan the target on radar. A good contact was achieved and the target was splashed (killed) at 47,000 ft. We went back to cruise power, carried out a gentle descent to 35,000 ft briefly enjoying the clear weather, well spattered with stars, but no moon, the night was really very dark.

I was beginning to think that we would now be allowed to recover to base when another target was allocated. They did ask whether we had sufficient fuel for one more interception, which we did (just). This one was at low level, apparently bent on attacking our base, so a rapid descent was required. I came back on the power to idle/fast idle, selected hot air (to prevent cockpit icing obscuring our view) and airbrakes and with gravity on our side we were soon plunging into the cloud layer at 30,000 ft – levelling around 60 seconds later at 2,000 ft. Searching for our third target, we were vectored towards the intruder and finally caught it flying at 500 ft still some 15 miles from the coast. This had to be a 'guns' kill as I had used both missiles on the first two interceptions. Closing in with a degree of care, I finally made visual contact at around 200 yards – a Canberra bomber, success number three.

We were now cleared to recover. Easing up to 3,000 ft prior to intercepting the ILS, we were cleared into the approach pattern, but by now we were getting low on fuel so the first approach had to count. Rain was still falling as we broke out of the overcast at around 800 ft, the runway lights, as always a welcome sight, came into view, and 50 minutes after rolling we touched down. Taxiing back to dispersal I asked the student what he had thought of the sortie but he was remarkably quiet for some time. Eventually, as we were walking back to Squadron Ops, he looked at me, shook his head and said that there was no way he could ever do a sortie like that. From take-off to recovery he reckoned he never caught up with what was going on, even though I told him as much as I could, bearing in mind the fact that my work load was high and I had little time to chat. I did make the point that he would not undertake a mission of that nature for quite some time to come, but it did give him food for thought as he progressed through the course. Some months later he successfully completed the conversion and weapons phases and departed to join his first operational squadron, but his first 'real' sortie in a Lightning certainly made quite an impression!

Having been promoted to the rank of Wing Commander, Peter Vangucci returned to operational flying in early 1972 as OC 19(F) Squadron flying Lightning F.2As at Gutersloh in Germany.

My next flying tour began in March 1972 in command of 19(F) Squadron at Gutersloh, only 65 miles from the Inner German border, or the Iron Curtain as it was known. We were the first line of defence with round-the-clock alert status which we shared with our sister squadron (Number 92). I suppose if such a rich cake could have any icing it would be the chance to fly the F.2A. By many, including me, this is reckoned to have been the best of all the Lightnings. It had the big ventral tank and therefore more fuel, which gave a disproportionate increase in flexibility. Hour-long sorties were an everyday occurrence and an hour and a quarter could be reached without having to think too much about saving fuel.

The 30 mm Aden guns had been retained in the nose, unlike the F.6, where they had had to be re-inserted into the front of the ventral tank, so with the F.2A there was no loss of fuel or gun harmonization problems. The cockpit contained the old analogue instrumentation, which made the generating of AC power less of a safety issue. All in all, the engines, the reheat, the controls and the general performance of the F.2A just made it 'feel' right, indeed the best. This was most noticeable because, as a result of some very wise and long-sighted staff work, HQ RAF Germany allowed us to practise air-to-air combat to very realistic limits, at which time all the F.2A's attributes seemed to come together. The squadron also had two of the old F.2s which, although avoided on exercise because of fuel shortage, were an absolute joy for a 'free' singleton sortie during which one could throw it all over the sky with gay abandon.

Shortly before becoming tour-expired in May 1974, Peter Vangucci led four 19 Squadron Lightning F.2As as the UK's participation in a flypast over Brussels on 4 April to mark the 25th anniversary of NATO. It was carried out in typical north European weather, which was to cause a few problems:

We deployed to Kleine Brogel on 3 April for a briefing and rehearsal. The Americans were leading the formation and also had a representative four. We were in alphabetical order, so we (the UK) were next to last, with only the US four behind us. Briefed height was not below 1,000 ft. We carried out stream take-offs in fours at 30-second intervals followed by a procedure-timed turn whether in contact with the preceding four or not. The flypast was to be in fours stepped down, line astern. The rehearsal went tolerably well in good visibility although some fours were so far below the one in front that we at the back end were definitely below 1,000 ft.

On the actual day we had the usual Belgian crud, with visibility into sun about zero and down sun about half a mile if you were lucky. We took off behind a nation that shall remain anonymous and I quickly made contact with them. Almost immediately afterwards I realized that the leader of the four in front had not turned on his time so were now detached from the rest of the formation. He called that he was lost so I checked with the Americans, made a turn, climbed a little for safety and said I was trying to re-establish contact with the formation. We opened out so that four pairs of eyes could look, but it seemed hopeless. Suddenly, just as the formation leader said he was on the timing limit to depart, I saw them all right underneath us. I warned the Americans as I dared not take my eyes off the formation and rolled down to join up. Fortunately all stayed with me (I had picked the best) and we joined up in line astern.

Settling into formation on the other fours seemed like a relaxing picnic after all that had gone before until I realized that some of those ahead were adding extra feet clearance due to the bad visibility and we were even lower than during the rehearsal. The leader called Brussels and gave the time to the flypast. I took a look sideways and was somewhat alarmed to see buildings going past at eye level with nasty TV masts sticking up above the level of my wing. From then on I had one eye on the formation and one eye looking for obstructions. The flypast went on time without further incident and looked pretty good, or so we heard, although I doubt whether anyone saw it for more than a few seconds! For the next few days every time the telephone rang I expected it to be HQ RAFG asking for an explanation as to why I was flying over Brussels at roof-top height. It never came – only a message that the C-in-C was pleased, thank goodness!

On 22 May 1974 Peter Vangucci flew the RAF's last-ever sortie in a Lightning F.2 when he carried out a short low-level aerobatic display over Gutersloh in XN794. For maximum effect he flew the entire sequence in reheat. Despite taking off with full internal fuel, his airborne time had to be rounded UP to 10 minutes when the flight was recorded in his logbook! He sums up the Lightning as follows:

Almost everyone who flew the Lightning loved it. It was a demanding aircraft, of that there is no doubt. The cockpit workload when operating the aircraft as a full weapons platform was pretty horrendous. Some pilots simply couldn't make it and failed the course. Others treated it with less than the respect it deserved and paid with their lives, the ultimate penalty. And that leads to the most surprising – and to many of us most perplexing – fact about the Lightning: its accident rate was worse than that of the Lockheed F-104 Starfighter, the one the Germans called the 'widow maker'. Fortunately all the bad publicity attracted by the Starfighter kept attention away from the Lightning, and to this day most people are unaware of this fact.

Sqn Ldr Mike Shaw also considered the F.2A to be his favourite Lightning, and got the chance to fly one during a tour at Boscombe Down:

While at Boscombe I was responsible for the annual updating of Pilot's Notes and Flight Reference Cards for all marks of Lightning and the writing of same for the yet-to-be-delivered F-4K and F-4M Phantoms (FG.1 and FGR.2). We had a Hunter F.6,

Meteor T.7, Canberra T.4 and Anson C.19 (!) to fly to keep our hands in, but in July/August 1967 I was checked out at Coltishall in the Lightning T.5. Eight hours in fourteen trips (that tells a story) and a horrible right-hand seat with the throttles on the right (in a fighter?).

Later that year a Lightning F.6 came my way (XP693). Eleven hours in eight trips, two with overwing tanks, but the best was kept to last – an F.2A. On 3 January 1968 I collected XN789 from Warton. Before delivery of this, the first for the RAF, I was to take it right round its cleared flight envelope. On take-off from Warton, both burners lit and all seemed well, but when I glanced down for the strip ASI, it wasn't there! The F.2A had the old (better in my view) round dial, and once located, it confirmed that I was lifting off at 175 kts IAS, so no harm was done. That is what comes of polluting my Lightning flying with T.5s, the F.6 and, four years previously, the F.3.

The F.2A was quiet as the long belly tank deadened noise from the forward engine. It had plenty of fuel, frugal engines (Avon 200s rather than 300s) and two Aden cannon in the fuselage. It had the cambered, extended leading edges of the F.6 and even at a higher AUW handled as well as the F.1, which was second only to the Hunter. After five sorties, including a run to Mach 1.7, I reluctantly ferried XN789 to Gutersloh on 15 January 1968 for handover to Sqn Ldr Laurie Jones, OC 19 Squadron. It was to be, as I knew then, the last time I would ever fly a Lightning. Truly, it was the unmatched Queen of the Skies.

When the Lightning first entered RAF service no-one could have envisaged that it would remain in first-line operational use for 28 years. Although few aircraft could match its performance, the limitations of the Lightning as a weapons system were gradually exposed over a period of time as newer fighters emerged. Trevor MacDonald-Bennett assesses the Lightning's capabilities:

At the inception of the Lightning the main emphasis was on sheer performance to counter any high-flying threat to the UK by manned bombers in all weathers. I would say that it succeeded in achieving that status very well, but at the expense of frighteningly short endurance, a very light weapons load, and a high workload for the pilot. The Lightning's performance and superb handling characteristics are of course legendary, but as the role rapidly changed and developed, many opportunities to develop the aircraft in sympathy with the ever-changing threat were sadly lost through the inertia of those in high places. Improvements came in the form of increased fuel capacity in the F.6, Red Top provided a head-on capability against supersonic targets and minor improvements were made to the radar. However, the insane decision to remove the guns from the F.3 took a long time before it was eventually reversed and they were reintroduced to the F.6. (I despair when I see that they have done exactly the same thing to the British version of Eurofighter purely on cost and political considerations.) So we stumbled on with a low-endurance aircraft with out-of-date radar, poor armament, poor visual lookout and very high single-seat workload.

If the will had been there the Lightning could have been radically improved by developing a new Doppler radar, doubling the quantity and mix of missiles such as Sidewinder and Sparrow (later developments of which were far superior to our infra-red only Firestreak and Red Top) and designing a new clear canopy to improve lookout. Our pulsed radar had very limited capability in the increasingly more complex low-level role, and I think I speak for the majority in expressing limited confidence in our missiles. Although we were fiercely proud of our 'single-seat' status, it would have been hard to oppose the idea of a developed two-seat variant based on the Saudi and Kuwaiti T.55 incorporating the above concepts. Much as I loved every moment of my time flying this most exciting, iconic aircraft, I reluctantly have to conclude that it was surpassed by the F-4 in every aspect as a weapons system.

The Lightning was also an engineering nightmare, and I have the highest regard for the engineers and technicians who worked so hard to keep us up and flying. It also suffered from the RAF obsession of stick-mounted hand braking, which meant that in strong crosswinds most of the braking action came from one brake only since almost full rudder was required to counteract the weathercock effect of the large fin and drag chute. Landing on or near the crosswind limit inevitably meant a wheel change on one side. With toe-mounted systems full braking could be applied to both wheels, even with full rudder deflection.

In the mid 1960s the Lightning was belatedly developed as a multi-role fighter, which is really what it should have been all along. Based on the F.6 with enlarged ventral fuel tank and cambered leading edges, the F.53 export version was capable of carrying a mix of conventional stores, including forty-four 2 in spin-stabilized rockets in twin retractable launchers, Matra 155 launchers housing eighteen SNEB 68 mm rockets or 1,000 lb bombs. The use of self-contained weapons packs allowed the F.53 to be reconfigured as an interceptor with Firestreak/Red Top missiles in less than an hour. The F.53 and two-seat T.55 were sold to Saudi Arabia and Kuwait. Having left the RAF in 1972, Trevor MacDonald-Bennett was to spend four years in Saudi Arabia:

I had planned to take up a career in civil aviation but found that I still hadn't quite got 'fun flying' out of my system. I was therefore very lucky to find myself in the position of Chief Weapons Instructor at Dhahran on the east coast of Saudi Arabia – initially with Airwork Ltd for a short period, then with BAC. Airwork had pioneered the very difficult Saudi contract but had lost the position on renewal. Serviceability was a major problem when I arrived, but BAC made big improvements under the watchful eye of a 'defence liaison team' of RAF personnel who carefully monitored engineering practices and mediated should there be any conflict between BAC and the Saudis.

The Lightning F.53 had a secondary ground-attack role with capability to fire 30 mm Aden cannon, 2 in rockets via two retractable doors under the nose, SNEB rockets mounted on wing pylons and 1,000 lb bombs dropped from the same pylons. The general course syllabus pretty much mirrored that in the UK, but the increased fuel capacity of the T.55 was a huge improvement. We enjoyed a very good relationship with the Royal Saudi Air Force commanders, who were generally open to suggestions and ideas. As long as diplomacy and tact were employed we were also well supported in matters arising from student progress in our rather unusual role as civilian instructors working in a military environment. Most importantly we all got on well both socially and professionally.

The course culminated in the ground-attack phase, which was very demanding and relatively risky as well as being heavy on fatigue life (aircraft and instructors!). At least one dual-range qualification sortie was flown with each student in the T.55 to learn and safely demonstrate all the range profiles. The T.55 had no real air-to-ground capability, so this was predominantly a safety exercise for the student to show him accurate flying and an awareness of the proximity of the ground during pull-ups from attack profiles. It also gave us the opportunity to demonstrate that one steady 'g' application was sufficient during this manoeuvre rather than multiple 'threepenny-bit' alternatives which severely punished the fatigue life of the aircraft. A typical sortie thereafter would comprise an instructor leading two students firing guns combined with SNEB 2 in rockets or 1,000 lb bombs. It was very demanding monitoring the students round the pattern as well as making one's own passes. The phase would conclude with two low-level cross-country exercises (led by the students), ending with 'attacking' the range and delivering all weapons in two passes.

The air-to-ground phase was my favourite part of the course, but also the most nerve wracking. I'm relieved to say that we never lost an aircraft on the range, but I recall the range safety officer ordering a student off the range after a VERY low pull out. On his return to base a 30 mm ricochet round was found lodged in the inlet guide vanes of the lower engine – an extremely lucky chap! This phase was also especially intensive for the armourers, who always went the extra mile. We invariably held a party in recognition of their efforts at the conclusion of the phase.

The Lightning performed amazingly well in this role. Even with our very basic sighting system the aircraft's great stability resulted in some very creditable scores, much to the frustration and annoyance of the American F-5 instructors with their far more sophisticated systems, whom we regularly beat!

Flying generally was very fatiguing, especially during the summer months when temperatures could reach 45° C. We would start early in the morning and finish by midday as the skin temperatures of the aircraft made them virtually untouchable. The air-conditioning system on the Lightning was also very poor, with cooling air only really becoming available as the aircraft climbed through medium levels. On range sorties one never really flew above 2,000 ft so these were particularly exhausting. It was also necessary to close the canopy prior to switching on the radar, which meant taxiing with virtually no airflow to the cockpit. Since Dhahran was at that time a joint civil/military airfield we had strict maximum start-up to airborne times to counter the very real and serious risk of dehydration, as in a protracted wait at the holding point for landing civil traffic.

Overall I thoroughly enjoyed my four years in Saudi Arabia – the aircraft were superbly maintained by a large group of like-minded expats and performed remarkably well, and the Saudis generally allowed us to get on with the job with very few irritating restraints. In the weapons sense I was effectively my own boss. We had plenty of continuation flying in the F.53s with virtual carte blanche in what we did and, dare I say, not a single frustrating senior RAF officer in sight! All in all it was a great way to finish eleven years with this magnificent aeroplane. The salary was pretty good too!

Although the Lightning was designed in an era when short-field performance was not even a consideration, given the right conditions and a light load it could be airborne in a surprisingly short distance. Brian Carroll relates an incident in Saudi Arabia in which freak weather conditions allowed a successful landing to be carried out at an entirely inappropriate airfield and a ferry flight that required fine judgement:

I took off in the late morning on a weather check, horizontal visibility was around 2,000 yards in blowing sand, though looking straight down the ground was easily seen from 30,000 ft. As a result I cleared a solo student to fly an instrument sortie and he took off twenty minutes after me. He was briefed to operate in an area 50–80 nm south-west of base. Forty minutes after he took off a radio call was heard from him declaring that he was lost. Radar was unable to locate him and as I was still airborne I attempted to get a bearing, but this too failed, due to the fact that he was approximately 240 nm away in the wrong direction. The weather conditions in his area were worse than in our authorized flying space, there was very limited contact with the ground and his air navigation system would not lock on due to his extreme range from base. By now I was getting low on fuel and had to recover.

I had only been back in operations a short while when the phone rang, and by then 90 minutes had passed since he got airborne. At the other end was my missing student, safe and sound on the ground at a rather obscure airfield close to the Kuwait border. A small Japanese oil company operated there and had a short runway used by light aircraft supplying them with basic essentials. We shall never know what forces came into play that allowed him to make a successful landing: the runway was too short, too soft, and yet from somewhere a surface wind sprang up blowing at 70 knots straight down the runway. The aircraft, having come to rest, then sank wheel deep into the macadam, and the strong wind faded away.

Meanwhile, a C-130 Hercules, which had been scrambled from Riyadh to conduct a search, was now instructed to land at Dhahran to fly a support crew to this airfield, now identified as Kafji. The name may be familiar to some, as it was to hit the headlines during the invasion of Kuwait and was the furthest the Iraqis penetrated into Saudi Arabia. The C-130 was loaded with essential equipment and spares, a number of ground crew were rounded up to join the party, and the Base Commander asked me if I would go with them and fly the aircraft back, always assuming it proved to be feasible.

Even from the cockpit of a C-130 the Kafji runway looked incredibly short; it was in fact 3,300 ft of soft, undulating tarmac, totally unsuitable for a Lightning. Parking up, we then inspected the aircraft and saw that it was anchored in the tarmac to a depth of around 18–24 inches. We were well received by the local emir, and overnight accommodation was arranged while decisions were made as to whether the aircraft could be flown out successfully. In ideal conditions a Lightning, given all its thrust, can get airborne in quite short distances. An F.6/F.53 will unstick in 2,700 ft using full reheat, an AUW of 38,500 lb (full internal fuel), an ambient temperature of +16° C, a 20 kt headwind and a runway elevation of 2,000 ft. Here we had a whole new ball game. The runway was only just long enough, and although a 2,700 ft ground run looks pretty good when you have 10,000 ft or more to start with, when the runway in question is only 3,300 ft long it is quite a different kettle of fish.

The following morning, after all the wheels and brake units had been changed and the aircraft partly refuelled, it was towed to a position on the PSP (metal sheeting) at the extreme end of the runway. Decision time had arrived: could I get airborne with an ambient air temperature of +30° C and the merest zephyr of a breeze? At least Kafji is at sea level, which was a slight bonus. I had already calculated the parameters the previous evening, and with full fuel I would have needed 3,600 ft to get airborne, so something had to go. Full internal fuel was acceptable, but the ventral load would have to be reduced. Another problem was the fact that my recovery airfield was 175 nm away. As the weather at Dhahran was such that I would have to make an instrument recovery, this would add another 54 nm to the overall distance, making a total of 229 nm. A fine balance was now needed to ensure that the aircraft could achieve lift-off on the short runway, but also that it had enough fuel to get home. Total aircraft weight was reduced by 3,600 lb, which left me with around 1,200 lb of fuel in the ventral tank.

Performance charts were examined several times to make sure that the calculations were correct. Crash crews were not available so that in the event that the aircraft failed to get airborne in the space available, I planned to eject and leave it to its own devices. The C-130 was at the upwind end of the runway, watching my take-off with interest. Afterwards the crew told me that I had a few feet to spare, probably into double figures, but they were not too sure. They also found that the whole exercise generated a high flow of adrenaline, and they were only watching!

Mention should also be made of the fact that local dignitaries were in attendance to watch my departure. All our pleading to keep farther away from the aircraft (they were within five feet of the wingtips) fell on deaf ears, or at least they were about to be deaf once engines were running and the reheat engaged. Rumour has it that they all fell over as I engaged reheat and began to roll, disappearing in my own mobile dust storm. The ground crew lost all sight of the aircraft until it finally emerged above the horizon after several tense moments. At least my calculations were correct, I was airborne.

I had a range potential in still air of 235 nm, which gave me a whole 6 nm to spare. By making a cruise descent I could save a few hundred pounds of fuel, even so it made for an interesting sortie, even more so as the weather deteriorated while *en route*, with visibility falling to 1,000 yards in blowing sand. The 30 minute flight back was fine apart from a main instrument and a services pressure (hydraulic) failure when I was still some 80 nm out from Dhahran. The weather at base was now RED, which really meant that it was unfit to take off, let alone land. Dhahran instructed me to divert to Bahrain, but I declined due to lack of fuel, and successfully landed with the assistance of ground radar and my onboard ILS. We never found out why or how the student found himself so far north of his briefed area, and as for the 70 kt wind, that remained very much an unknown as well.

CHAPTER FIFTEEN

The Lightning Compared

W hen it entered service with 74 Squadron in July 1960, few other aircraft could match the Lightning in terms of performance, and it was to retain this pre-eminent position until the emergence of the next generation of interceptor fighters, such as the General Dynamics F-16 Fighting Falcon and McDonnell Douglas F-15 Eagle, in the mid-1970s. This chapter compares the Lightning with some of its rivals.

DASSAULT MIRAGE III

The Mirage III was a close contemporary of the Lightning and was first flown in prototype form on 17 November 1956. A team from A&AEE evaluated the pre-production Mirage IIIA in January 1960, the pilots being Sqn Ldr Alan Merriman and Flt Lt Lou Cockerill, who had both been involved in Lightning development at Boscombe Down. The handling characteristics of the Mirage IIIA were well liked, although severe restrictions imposed as a result of concern about inertia coupling, pilot-induced oscillations (PIOs) below 200 kts IAS, undesirable trim changes on application of air brake, and stall/spin considerations were a little disappointing. The cockpit layout and clearview hood were considered excellent, but a lack of nosewheel steering detracted from the aircraft's manoeuvrability on the ground. The handling characteristics of the Atar engine were good with the exception of its slow thrust response when on the approach. In conjunction with this feature, the over-sensitivity of longitudinal control and the steep nose-up attitude made the approach the least satisfactory region of flight to be experienced.

The engineering design of the Mirage III was highly praised, its excellence having already been reflected in good serviceability. Considerable care had also been shown as regards simplifying the pilot's operation of the aircraft, although it was felt that further development was required on cockpit conditioning and windscreen and canopy demisting. In conclusion, the fact that the Mirage III was likely to be one of the world's leading supersonic fighters was recognized in the Boscombe Down report, as was its adaptability – its relative simplicity, small size and low-pressure tyres allowing it to be operated from a variety of airfield surfaces in a number of alternative roles.

The production version, the Mirage IIIC, was flown by Wg Cdr David Simmons during an exchange posting in 1960, a time when he was evaluating the Lightning with AFDS at Coltishall:

In July 1960 I did a Lightning/Mirage exchange with Cdt Franchi of CEAM at Mont de Marsan. I had three flights on the Mirage IIIC, which included accelerating to 1.9 M at 36,000 ft. It turned out to be slightly disappointing as it was very noisy and shook like hell! Fuel could disappear more quickly than in a Lightning and flight times were only 25–35 minutes. In July 1961 I flew to Istres to conduct a series of trials on the Mirage IIIO equipped with a Rolls-Royce Avon engine with a con-di efflux. The Australians were buying Mirages to replace their Avon-Sabres. The Avon had a better performance than the SNECMA engine (Atar), with superior specific fuel consumption. This forced SNECMA to over-speed their engines to try to match it. I also did one ferry trial with oversize underwing drop tanks. I felt as if I was balanced on a pinhead after take-off. I went round and round France and reck-oned that I could have flown from the UK to Cyprus without refuelling. This flight lasted 2 hours 25 minutes. The Lightning's reaction and time to height beat the lot for high-level targets, and its weapons system was better than the Mirage, but for low-level targets it had some limitations.

Trevor MacDonald-Bennett also had plenty of opportunities to assess the Mirage III during his first tour with 74 Squadron at Tengah in the late 1960s:

The Royal Australian Air Force at that time had Mirages based at Butterworth near Penang in Malaysia. This presented superb opportunities for reciprocal detachments with regular Lightning visits to Butterworth, and Mirages to Tengah. I was lucky enough to fly the two-seater a couple of times, and additionally we flew regular sorties against them. I found the Mirage to be a delight in terms of handling, but being a proper delta its low-speed drag characteristics were horrendous, making the need to keep speed and energy levels high in a turning scenario even more crucial than with the Lightning. This, of course, is because of the inefficient change of wing section with elevons deflected up, whereas the Lightning's separate tailplane eliminated this delta characteristic. I also found it a bit of a 'jack of all trades but master of none', and certainly found the huge power levels of our own steed very comforting. I also think our radar was superior, but they had the very real advantage of gun armament (before the reintroduction of guns on the F.6). Another surprising omission was the absence of in-flight refuelling capability, and I believe that the Australians found any form of significant deployment a major logistical nightmare. Notwithstanding all the above, it seemed a very simple, practical machine and was well liked by all who flew it. Maintenance-wise it left the Lightning for dead, with service-ability levels way ahead of ours in spite of the huge efforts put in by our groundcrews.

We flew everything from radar intercepts, 1 v. 1, 2 v. 2, and up to 4 v. 4 (when we had enough serviceable aircraft!), and overall we were pretty evenly matched. We had a theoretical advantage in out-and-out performance terms, but this could very easily be lost by superior flying by the opposition if we were not careful. They certainly enjoyed a better lookout, but one surprising factor was fuel consumption. Most high 'g' combat situations, even when started at high level, very quickly end up at medium levels in thicker air where more thrust is available. An unusual characteristic of the Lightning reheat system was a relatively small thrust increment of about 30 per cent above cold power. In comparison the cold power/reheat ratio of the Phantom was around 55 per cent, the Mirage being in the order of 45 per cent. Combining this with the delta-wing drag characteristics meant almost continuous use of reheat by the Mirage, whereas the Lightning could use it selectively in combination with cold power once the dogfight had reached these lower levels. The net result was very similar 'chicken out' times for both types in spite of the Mirage's apparent superior fuel capability with drop tanks fitted.

Convair F-102/F-106

The F-102A Delta Dagger, powered by one 11,700 lb s.t. Pratt and Whitney J57, entered squadron service with the USAF in 1956 and was used for mainland defence and by units based in Europe and in the Pacific region. David Simmons also flew the F-102A and was able to evaluate its performance as regards reheat climbs and interception techniques. In addition he was able to participate in a major exercise. He considered the F-102 to have reheat performance roughly comparable to the Lightning in cold power, but was impressed by the aircraft's weapons system and appreciated the fact that sorties of the order of 1 hour 30 minutes could be flown on internal fuel. His overall assessment was that it was a good, solid aircraft with a relatively roomy cockpit.

The F-106 Delta Dart was a development of the F-102 and featured a Pratt and Whitney J75 rated at 17,200 lb s.t. It entered service in the summer of 1959 and was tested around that time by a team from Britain that included Sqn Ldr Alan Merriman (A&AEE), Wg Cdr Jimmy Dell (CFE) and Lt Cdr J.T. Humphreys (RAE). The aircraft flown were two-seat F-106Bs, which apart from the additional tandem seating position were identical to the single-seat F-106A. A total of nine flights were made from Edwards AFB and the team's conclusions were as follows:

In general the aircraft had good handling qualities when the yaw and pitch dampers were operative, but with the dampers inoperative there was an appreciable deterioration of the handling qualities. To consider the aircraft's good and bad points in more detail, it will be convenient to follow a typical flight sortie. The time to close the canopy was excessive and so also was the time required to start the engine. The lack of a parking brake was soon apparent. The ground handling was good and the method of selecting nosewheel steering much liked, but the idling thrust was too high and accentuated the non-progressive nature of the wheel braking. The elevator power was good in the take-off and no difficulties with regard to control were experienced in this phase of flight after the initial period of familiarization.

The flying controls were well harmonized in all flight conditions and the longitudinal trim rate was particularly good. On the other hand, the dynamic stability was not good even with the dampers operative, a feature which was particularly noticeable in the pitching plane even in general flying. With the dampers off, there was an appreciable deterioration, which was most noticeable in the lateral mode, particular trouble being experienced with the undamped and quite violent rolling oscillations which occurred at various flight speeds. Also noticeable were random small lateral changes of trim. The manoeuvrability in terms of 'g' available before the onset of buffeting was only moderate, though it appeared that there was a relatively large reserve of available lift which could be used if the onset of buffet could be delayed.

The airbrakes were comparatively ineffective with a nose-up

trim change at some conditions. The engine handling was not of the standard expected on British aircraft. The warning system was not visible in sunlight and was illogical in having several major warning lights not on the main panel. The permanently live microphone was an annoying distraction and the need was felt of an indication of engine inlet vari-ramp position. The fuel gauging appeared generally good in not having indicator oscillations, but there were some changes (up to 300 lb) in indications with quite large attitude changes. The landing parachute was not particularly effective and the lack of an anti-skid device for wheel braking was not liked. The performance in level flight at maximum thrust, without reheat, was mainly subsonic and the performance with reheat was not outstanding in the prevailing temperature conditions when compared with that of some other modern single-seat aircraft.

Lockheed F-104 Starfighter

Of all the American Century-series fighters, the F-104 Starfighter was perhaps the closest to the Lightning in terms of its climb rate and speed, but its design was radically different. It was a product of experience gained during the Korean War and was an attempt to deliver out-and-out performance from a lightweight airframe and a single reheated General Electric J79 turbojet. The Starfighter had a troubled development – a number of aircraft crashed because of various engine maladies, and handling difficulties were experienced with the high-set tail, which suffered 'pitch-up' and some of the first instances of a stable 'superstall', a condition that was to afflict a number of 'T-tailed' airliners in the 1960s, in which the tail surfaces were rendered ineffective owing to blanketing by the wing. The small, highly loaded wing had blown flaps to increase lift in the approach configuration and reduce touchdown speed to a reasonable 165 kts IAS. Undoubtedly one of the main factors that led to a high fatality rate during Starfighter development was the use of a downward-firing ejection seat to avoid the possibility of the pilot hitting the tail. Roland Beamont flew an early F-104A in June 1958 and recorded his experiences in his book, *Testing Years* (Ian Allan, 1980). Although his comments may contain a certain bias, his views on the F-104 were obviously shared by others, as it saw only limited service with the United States Air Force.

The F-104 was a small, rough-engined aeroplane with good basic longitudinal characteristics, neutral lateral static stability with inadequate directional damping characteristics, which gave a persistent low-amplitude, short-period oscillation with rudder autostabilizer engaged that became divergent with autostabilizer off at high Mach number. The 104's most unsatisfactory feature was the severe effect of its minimal-area, highly loaded and very thin supersonic wing on turning manoeuvrability. When attempting to manoeuvre Lightning-style at any speed below 500 kts, the 104 was extremely limited by buffet and stick-jerker. It was clear beyond doubt that the manoeuvrability of this aircraft was far less than the standard expected of a conventional fighter.

None the less, on the third flight it was exhilarating to accelerate out to Mach 2, albeit with delicate throttle handling to guard against the briefed sensitivity to surge and flame-out. There was also heavy aerodynamic vibration and noise as the ASI approached 700 kts, with a large green 'SLOW' light flashing on the central warning panel to indicate that limiting recovery temperature (120° C) was not far away. From these flights it was obvious that although the Starfighter was an intriguing design and a successful attempt at achieving Mach 2 performance with the power of one readily available series-production engine, it had a number of serious drawbacks to operational capability. I felt that it had one of the best examples of fighter cockpit design that I had come across. Apart from that and the excellent vision through windscreen and canopy and its high performance, it had little to commend it as a modern fighter interceptor. Still less was it suitable for its future role as a tactical strike aeroplane.

Following its initial failure to attract substantial orders, the Starfighter was transformed into a low-level strike aircraft with a secondary air-defence capability as the F-104G and was sold widely throughout the world. During one of the early 'Tiger Meets' at Leuchars in 1966 the opportunity was taken to compare the Starfighter's level acceleration with that of a Lightning F.3, and it was found that, despite each aircraft having temporary advantage at various stages, they reached their limiting IAS at almost identical times. In terms of air combat manoeuvring, however, the Lighting was superior, one Lightning pilot commenting that this was not particularly surprising as Lockheed had forgotten to put wings on their machine!

The F-104 was to achieve notoriety, especially in West Germany, as the result of an extremely high loss rate, and although the Lightning was to match it in 1970/1 with seventeen write-offs in a twenty-month period, the Starfighter's problems existed over a much longer timescale. In 1962 the *Luftwaffe* lost an F-104 for every 720 hours flown. Another characteristic was that in a high proportion of these accidents the pilot lost his life (of the Lightning losses mentioned above, five resulted in a fatality). Although the F-104's accident rate had dropped to slightly more 'acceptable' levels by the early 1970s, it never really managed to shake off the nickname 'Widow maker', first coined after its traumatic introduction into service.

McDonnell Douglas F-4 Phantom

In September 1964, having flown 350 sorties (but only 250 hours) on Lightning F.1s with 74 Squadron, Mike Shaw commenced a two-year exchange posting with the US Marine Corps on F-4B Phantoms. He subsequently commanded the Phantom OCU (No. 228) at Coningsby, and is thus well qualified to comment on the characteristics of the two aircraft.

I first flew the F-4B Phantom in 1964, about two months after leaving 74 Squadron at Leuchars, which was then re-equipping with Lightning F.3s after four years with F.1s. The Phantom was a development of the F-3 Demon, a single-seat, single-engine naval fighter, and the F-101 Voodoo, a twin-engined, two-seat all-weather fighter for the US Air Force. It had two J79 General Electric afterburning turbojets, a Westinghouse pulse radar (APQ-72) and a sturdy airframe by McDonnell Douglas; it had almost twice the Lightning F.1's internal fuel and could carry three drop tanks, bringing its total capacity to 22,000 lb. In addition, it could carry up to eight guided weapons (four Sparrow IIIs plus four Sidewinders). The F-4B had no internal gun, but nor did the Lightning F.3, unlike the F.1, F.2, F.2A, and some F.6s.

The Lightning did not match the Phantom as a weapon, or in range or endurance, but because it was lighter and aero-dynamically cleaner, it handled very much better. The Phantom came into US Navy service only two years after the F-4H's first flight, and compared with the Lightning was less refined as a flying machine. It had autostabilization on all three axes (pitch, roll and yaw), all selected by a single magnetically held switch, so a momentary interruption of electrical power could lead to a wild ride! Further, the roll channel would 'fight back', making a smooth roll impossible. Later F-4s had three separate locking switches, so roll could be switched off. Pitch was always needed, particularly at aft CG.

Pitch trim was unhappy too, as the stick position moved with trim. This meant that as the F-4B accelerated, the pilot would find that he was trimming the stick further and further away from him. At high subsonic speed, the pilot could not then rest his wrist on his knee, so stick movement involved his whole arm. As one inch of stick movement could generate up to 6 g, this was not comfortable, and delicate pitch control was difficult. Worse, the cheap and nasty plastic stick top had a circular force-transducer spring contact which allowed it to move about an eighth of an inch in any direction without effect on the flight controls. This all made likely a pilot-induced oscillation (PIO), when the pilot tried to damp out a pitch disturbance but would find that his arm had become an out-of-phase force function that actually made things worse. The Flight Manual stated that all high-speed aircraft were prone to this. Not the Lightning, nor any other aircraft cleared by Boscombe Down.

When supersonic, the nose-down pitch change brought the Phantom's stick back within easy reach, as did lowering of the flaps. At these times, the aircraft was delightful to fly; in between, however, it needed a lot more development. Its turning performance, too, had been sacrificed to the God of Mach 2, a speed hardly ever used. The Phantom, except those fitted with leading-edge slats, ran into pre-stall buffet whenever any serious back pressure was applied to the stick, although there was usually sufficient power from the responsive J-79s to overcome the drag. So, in combat manoeuvring, it was essential to keep speed and energy high and not to rely too much on turning performance, as the wings were too thin to provide much subsonic lift below about 450 kts IAS. In the approach or 'dirty' configuration, the F-4B was above criticism. The boundary layer control brought it in over 20 kts slower than the Lightning, and its hook was strong enough to hang up 4½ Phantoms! In short, as a weapon, give me the Phantom – but as a flying machine, the Lightning wins every time!

Not long after the Phantom entered service with the RAF, a non-stop deployment was made to Singapore to determine the viability of such operations at short notice. In addition this provided an excellent opportunity for dissimilar air combat training for 74 Squadron, the resident Lightning unit at Tengah. Trevor MacDonald-Bennett recalls his impressions of the exercise:

The 'trick cyclists' (RAF doctors) had a whale of a time assessing crew fatigue, blood sugar levels, etc. I remember meeting one particular Phantom crew comprising a very fit-looking young pilot who needed helping out of the cockpit, and his (relatively) geriatric-looking navigator whose first question was, 'When can I visit the bar?' On the operational side, the F-4 demonstrated its vastly superior deployment potential. It could navigate autonomously and rendezvous with tankers along the route (Lightnings were required to accompany the tankers), and it also had sufficient oxygen, oil, etc. for this sortie length (the Lightning was restricted to about ten hours due to oxygen capacity). We soon started to fly joint exercises with the F-4s, and in terms of sheer performance they seemed quite evenly matched. In the close-combat dog-fighting scenario the F-4 had a greater theoretical fuel capacity advantage, but in reality, rather like the Mirage, this was significantly reduced by their almost continuous need for reheat.

The real advantages of the F-4 revolved around the two-crew concept and a far superior weapons system: firstly, a pulse Doppler radar with good look-down capability, far greater range, and multiple target capability; secondly, a mix of radar-guided Sparrow and infra-red Sidewinder missiles, plus the fighter pilot's greatest friend – a gun. All this with the significantly reduced workload gained by most aspects of the system being controlled by the navigator, the far superior fuel capacity when used in its planned interceptor role, and a true long-range head-on capability using the Sparrows. The crew also had the benefit of a typical large, luxurious, well-ventilated American cockpit.

The excellent radar performance was perfectly demonstrated during an exercise involving a simulated strike from the north over Malaysia. F-4s flew north/south-orientated high-level race-track patterns well to the north and picked up low-flying high-speed 'enemy' Mirages while covering any high-altitude threat simultaneously. Approximate positions of the Mirages were passed to Lightnings flying mainly east/west-orientated CAPs (combat air patrols), and a significant number were detected in this way. The Lightning radar being pulsed only, and therefore severely affected by ground clutter, was close to useless in this environment. I reluctantly have to admit that the outcome would have been very different without the involvement of the Phantoms.

Notwithstanding all the above, several of the F-4 crews were old pals, and I recall one comment which made me feel a little better. In terms of pure exhilaration and fun flying he likened the F-4 to a Chevy Corvette and the Lightning to a Ferrari! I also understand that the F-4 very much depended on artificial stabilization to a far greater degree than the Lightning. In fact it was difficult to detect any difference with autostabilization off in the Lightning, but apparently at high IAS the F-4 was potentially very dangerous in similar configuration – especially in pitch.

SUBSONIC FIGHTERS

During his tour in the Far East, Trevor MacDonald-Bennett also flew air-combat sorties against a wide variety of subsonic types, including Javelin, Hunter, Sea Vixen, Buccaneer and A-4 Skyhawk:

> The Javelin was really past its 'sell-by date' and was quite restricted as a result of age and structural concerns. In fact there was a horrific fatal accident when one 'clapped wings' and disintegrated close to the airfield during a rolling high-g manoeuvre. About the only manoeuvre it could accomplish and cause us serious embarrassment was to break away vertically down with idle thrust and full airbrake – it was impossible for us not to overshoot unless we flew a high-g spiral around them. Hence the Javelin's nickname of 'dragmaster'! Fair comparisons are difficult to make, but the Lightning was highly superior in most respects, including the radar.
>
> The Hunter was a day-fighter/ground-attack aircraft with no airborne radar capability. In our primary air-defence role the need for close air combat should never arise as we would hopefully fire our weapons against such a target without him sighting us. However, it is an imperfect world so we did fly ACM sorties against Hunters to cover the situation where we had been seen prior to missile launch. We very soon learnt that trying to mix it with the Hunter (or any other subsonic aircraft) at their speeds and on their terms could prove disastrous, and in the early days a few embarrassing Hunter gunsight pictures of Lightnings proved the point. The secret was to retain our vastly superior energy levels by manoeuvring in the vertical plane using high- and low-speed 'yo-yo' techniques. Our most serious limitation in this scenario was lack of gun armament. Our Firestreak and Red Top missiles would have almost certainly been useless in this high-g environment, even assuming that one had been able to lock the radar to the target. However, approval to modify the F.6 with Aden cannon was known to be forthcoming, so we did train in this close-quarter environment, artificial though it was. Tengah's Hunter pilots were extremely talented and it was unusual to track one for long! Another distinct disadvantage for the Lightning was its limited visual lookout capability – far too much ironmongery

in the canopy. Our next serious limitation was fuel and endurance. In summary it was extremely difficult to manoeuvre into a 'kill' position behind a Hunter or similar subsonic aircraft, but it should have been impossible for them to get anywhere near a correctly flown Lightning employing the appropriate tactics.

We were very fortunate to receive regular Royal Navy detachments, allowing us to develop tactics against their aircraft. The Sea Vixen enjoyed the same role as ourselves with, I suspect, a slightly inferior radar and the same serious limitation of no guns. My own experience of ACM sorties against them demonstrated what seemed a slightly less agile aircraft than the Hunter, requiring almost identical tactics. They also enjoyed a much superior endurance and some very determined aircrew. How their observers stood the discomfort of all the violent manoeuvring from their 'black hole', with its one tiny window, I will never know. The Buccaneer was, of course, a very heavy, fast ultra-low-level strike aircraft, and opportunities to 'mix it' with them were not so frequent. They had no self-defence capability, but their low-level skills were superb and great caution was required when trying to turn with them during an attempted intercept as there was a very real risk of flying yourself into the ground or the sea. If they were caught out anywhere other than low level I felt they were no match for the Lightning's performance.

Additionally we enjoyed a period when Royal Australian Navy Skyhawks were based at Tengah during a cruise of their infamous carrier HMAS *Melbourne* (of regular collision fame!). I distinctly recall flying against them and becoming very frustrated, as I thought that at last I was in behind the opposition only to realize that it was the pointed end of the delta coming towards me – not the back end as I had thought! It appeared to turn extremely well, and being so small it was a difficult target to acquire visually. Again the secret was to retain energy levels.

McDONNELL DOUGLAS F-15 EAGLE

Any comparison between the F-15 and the Lightning might, at first, seem to be a little unfair, especially as the two designs are separated by twenty years, a similar timescale to that between the Sopwith Camel and the Supermarine Spitfire. Although the F-15 was clearly superior in terms of its radar capability and weapons load, when it came to handling and performance the Lightning was still liable to get one over on its younger adversary. Mike Shaw, by now a group captain, was one of the first Royal Air Force pilots to fly the F-15 Eagle in 1975, a time when the RAF might have purchased the aircraft for the Air Defence role had American airlines been interested in buying Concorde:

In April 1975 I was ordered to report to RAF Bentwaters for a one-day attachment. I was OC 228 OCU on Phantoms at the time, training crews for the Air Defence role, as the Spey-engined Phantom was replacing the Lightning. On arrival at Bentwaters, I found a TF-15A awaiting, a prototype making a demonstration tour of NATO Europe with an E-3 AWACS aircraft. I was to have a single rear-seat ride, as I knew nothing about the F-15 or its systems at that time. Col Smith was the pilot.

First impressions were very favourable, as the vision from the roomy cockpit was superb. So was the climb, the buffet-free turning performance and the clarity of the synthetic-display radar. We picked up two F-111 target aircraft, identified them using IFF and locked one up at over twice the range that I was used to, all directed and monitored by the E-3. The launch of a Sparrow triggered a countdown to 'impact', leaving time for the second F-111 to be similarly engaged. The demonstration was convincing, as I expected! But far better was to come.

In October 1975 I was sent to St Louis, Missouri, with two other pilots to evaluate the F-15 as an Air Defence fighter for the RAF. The team was led by Gp Capt John Tritton, and the other pilot was Sqn Ldr Roger Beasley, a test pilot from A&AEE Boscombe Down, which also sent two technical wizards. We spent a week with McDonnell Douglas (MDC) at St Louis doing a comprehensive ground school and using their 2 v. 1 combat fighter simulator. After being ferried by the company Learjet to Edwards AFB, California, we found TF-15A No. 71291 (the one that had come to Bentwaters) waiting for us.

I was given four sorties, all in the front seat, with MDC pilot Denny Behm in the back. After the first general handling trip Denny bravely left all the flying to me! On the next three days, MDC set up targets at my request, starting at medium level (5,000–30,000 ft), subsonic. The radar was very easy to use, and the TF-15 was so manoeuvrable that the targets (F-5s) proved to be no problem, particularly as they were briefed to fly as non-evading 'bombers'. The TF-15, with its very low wing-loading, turned smoothly, and even at 5 g without buffet, although the fan engines had to be kept at MIL power, i.e. 100 per cent rpm, whenever high angle of attack was applied. The head-up display was clear and steady, and target tracking was simple. The aircraft had none of the shortcomings of the Phantom, and was even more pleasant to fly than the Lightning, though no more exhilarating. But it was twenty years newer, with a magnificent weapons system and view – and fuel! Indeed we carried two conformal 'fast-pack' tanks, each with 3,000 lb of AVTUR. These were very useful when intercepting supersonic (M=1.6) F-4s the next day, but were not so good when it came to tackling supersonic high-fliers.

The final test was a low-level 'attack' by four F-5s, with the TF-15 on combat air patrol (CAP) at FL180. The fighter coped with all four, taking two head-on with Sparrows and two tail-on with Sidewinders, all on one 'converted' run. It was most impressive! In the event we did not sell Concorde in the USA, so a proposed deal to procure F-15s for the RAF fell through. It would have been a fine addition to our front line in the Air Defence role, but NATO won the Cold War anyway!

Brian Carroll also flew the F-15 when he was CFI with the Royal Saudi Air Force in the late 1970s:

My first impression of the F-15 Eagle was of its size – it was a large aircraft, bigger than the Lightning in every respect, especially inside the cockpit; so much room that one could nearly walk around compared to the glove-like fit of the Lightning. Even so, everything came to hand without having to stretch, in fact all essential control functions could be accessed from either the stick or the throttle. In all there were fifteen multi-function buttons and switches. Having said that, the Lightning, too, was well supplied with such facilities, though they were spread a little wider, and there were more of them. At least twenty-two primary ones and several others were scattered around various parts of the cockpit. There was a certain amount of rapid hand work needed from time to time, and considerable dexterity to ensure hitting the correct switch. Embarrassing if one was to switch the radar off at a critical moment. I never did!

Starting systems on both aircraft were straightforward, though taxiing out needed some braking since they would both gently accelerate if not held in check. Take-off acceleration in both was impressive, but the Lightning was quicker off the ground and reached climb speed of 450 kts in 61.8 seconds. The range of the F-15 was impressive – with three external tanks it could cover about 2,500 nm. Compare that to the Lightning's figures: on standard internal tanks (filling the over-wing tanks prior to take-off gave no advantage as the extra weight burned off so much fuel), the maximum attainable range was 900 miles. Even this was stretching things a bit and required a cruise let-down to conserve fuel.

My first F-15 flight involved a formation take-off, and here I discovered the first difference. The Pratt and Whitney engines (turbofans) were slow to react to throttle movement, so maintaining a steady position on the wing of my lead aircraft took a few moments to sort out, otherwise it presented no difficulties, and I was soon relaxed and enjoying the flight. Later F-15s had digital electronic engine control systems to allow faster response times to throttle demands. For the F-15, a typical training configuration weight was around 45,000 lb with a combat load of approximately 55,000 lb. This compares with a figure of 41,700 lb maximum take-off weight with full combat load in a Lightning F.53.

The brief for my sortie was a 1 v. 1 interception profile, followed by 1 v. 1 air combat manoeuvres (ACM). I now experienced a whole new world of avionics. This was where the Eagle was head and shoulders above its peers. The Eagle's avionics were centred around the APG-63 pulse Doppler radar. It also had a radar warning receiver which alerted the pilot to enemy radars in various modes. On the defensive side, the Eagle had a countermeasures dispenser which allowed it to deploy chaff and flares for its own protection. The Lightning's radar was, to say the very least, basic, and hard work to operate, and the phrase 'a one-armed paper hanger' comes to mind. The Lightning had no defensive countermeasures, something that we would have appreciated (some enterprising pilots occasionally carried chaff in the small amount of space available underneath the airbrakes, allowing a 'one-shot' capability when the airbrakes were opened). By comparison the F-15's kit was simplicity itself to use. All the requisite information to carry out an interception was displayed on the HUD. Details such as the target's speed and height were shown digitally, along with its heading. Should the target throw a turn, the display informed you of the direction of turn and also the amount of 'g' it was pulling. Pick-up range was far in excess of the Lightning's AI, and in the lower levels ground returns were virtually non-existent.

As regards weaponry, a typical F-15 combat load was 4 × AIM-120 AMRAAM, 2 × AIM-7 Sparrow, 2 × AIM-9 Sidewinder, plus 940 rounds of the internal 20 mm cannon. The Lightning was poorly armed, carrying only two missiles and two 30 mm cannons. The F.53 could also fit bombs and rockets, but its weapons load was no match for the F-15. Manoeuvrability in the

F-15 during 1 v. 1 combat was outstanding throughout the entire flight envelope from less than 100 knots to more than Mach 2.0, and I have no doubt that the Eagle would be more than a match for the Lightning. With so much thrust, optimum manoeuvring speed was easily maintained, with little if any need to unload in order to maintain it.

The overall impression was that both aircraft had very similar performance and handling characteristics. Both were a joy to fly. Considering the age difference, the Lightning's performance was totally outstanding when introduced into service, and when it finally bowed out it could still out-climb most of its successors. Given the choice between the F-15 and the Lightning, I would have been mad not to take the Eagle, but only because it had such superb avionics and weaponry. For the pure joy of flying, the Lightning still heads the list. It was, and indeed still is, a magnificent aircraft and a credit to the designers and test pilots who developed and brought it into service for people like me to enjoy.

Glossary

A&AEE	Aeroplane and Armament Experimental Establishment
AC	Alternating Current (electricity)
ACT	Air Combat Training
AFDS	Air Fighting Development Squadron
AI	Attitude Indicator, Airborne Interception (radar)
APC	Armament Practice Camp
ASI	Air Speed Indicator
CA Release	Controller Air Release
CEAM	Conférence des Ecoles et Académies Militaires européennes
CFE	Central Fighter Establishment
CG	Centre of Gravity
C_L	Lift Coefficient
DC	Direct Current (electricity)
ECM	Electronic Counter Measures
FL	Flight Level
GCA	Ground-Controlled Approach
GCI	Ground-Controlled Interception
GW	Guided Weapons
HI	Heading Indicator
HP Cock	High-Pressure Fuel Cock
IAS	Indicated Airspeed
IFF	Identification Friend or Foe
ILS	Instrument Landing System
IMN	Indicated Mach Number
IWI	Interceptor Weapons Instructor
JPT	Jet Pipe Temperature
LCS	Lightning Conversion Squadron
Maxaretting	Use of anti-skid control
MRG	Master Reference Gyro
PAS	Pilot Attack Sight

PIO	Pilot-Induced Oscillation
QFE	Atmospheric pressure at airfield elevation
QGH	Controlled Descent
QNH	Atmospheric pressure at sea level
QRA	Quick Reaction Alert
RB	Rocket Battery
RPM, rpm	Revolutions Per Minute
R/T	Radio Transmitter
SNEB	A type of 68mm unguided pod-launched rocket
SNECMA	Sociéte Nationale d'Etude et de Construction de Moteurs d'Aviation
SWP	Standard Warning Panel
TACAN	Tactical Air Navigation (navigation aid)
TMN	True Mach Number
TTC	Top Temperature Control
UHF	Ultra-High Frequency
VMC	Visual Meteorological Conditions
VHF	Very High Frequency
VSI	Vertical Speed Indicator
XC	Cross-Country (navigation)

Lightning F.1 and F.1A Flight Reference Cards – July 1961

COCKPIT CHECKS – EXTERNAL DC SUPPLY ONLY CONNECTED

* Applies to Mk.1 aircraft only
\+ Applies to Mk.1A aircraft only

Main armament safety break	Disconnected
GW arming switch	Off
Ejection seat	Check
Armament trigger safety catch	SAFE
Undercarriage down button	IN (UP button over-ride knobs horizontal)
Strap in	–
Engine starter master switch	ON
Battery switch	ON
Instrument master switch	ON (Roller blind erects after 20 sec)

COCKPIT – LOWER LEFT SIDE

Canopy operating lever	Up
Ram-air valve	CLOSED and locked
Canopy jettison handle	Fully down
Demist lever	OFF (Rear)

Throttle servo control	UNLOCK
Undercarriage emergency lever	Fully forward (safety wire unbroken) (Mk.1A – spring clip in position)
* VHF sets	On
+ UHF	Channel selected Function switch T/R Power switch – NORMAL
ILS master switch	OFF
ILS channel switch	As required
+ TACAN	ON Channel selected Aerial as required DIST/BRG or BRG as required
Ventral tank and missile jettison handle	Fully in. Trigger wired or guarded

COCKPIT – MIDDLE LEFT SIDE

+ Flight refuelling panel	Test lights, leave switch central
AI hand controller	Ground test switch inboard
Emergency canopy jack release	Outboard
Throttles	Fully forward, then idle/fast idle

COCKPIT – UPPER LEFT SIDE

SWP	Test. Check lights, audio, mute and cancel

COCKPIT – LEFT FRONT

Feel switch	ON
Feel indicator	ON
Undercarriage selector	DOWN
Undercarriage position indicator	3 green lights – alternate bulb – day/night switch
JPT controller switches	AUTO – wired
Autopilot trim indicator	Central
Combined trim indicator	Test trim switches individually for live circuit, then operate combined

	trim switches over full range. Set: Rudder – Neutral, Aileron – Neutral, Tailplane – TO
Braking parachute selector	Fully in
Slip indicator	Central
Anti-dazzle light switch	OFF
Accelerometer	Reset
Flaps	UP (indicating UP)
Standby art. horizon switch	NORMAL
Standby art. horizon	Flag showing
MRG NORMAL/FAST ERECTION switch	NORMAL
Standby inverter indicator	ON (white)
Flight instruments	Visual check
Emergency lamps switch	OFF
* Air diffuser control lever	As required
* Oxygen regulator NORMAL/100% switch Mask-jerkin Flow indicators	Contents – Full 200–400psi 100% TEST – Return to NORMAL Annunciating
* VHF indicators	Indicating channel selected
RPM indicators	Normal
JPT indicators	Normal
Fuel gauges	Contents
Ventral flow indicator	White
* TACAN	ON Channel selected Aerial switch (if fitted) as required
Camera control unit	Off
Armament selector switch	OFF
AVS flow control	As required
Anti-G cock	ON. Set L. or H. as required

COCKPIT – UPPER RIGHT SIDE

E2b COMPASS	Check
Canopy unlock warning lights	On

Armed time clock	Zero
Arming warning lights	Out
RB doors unlocked light	Out
RB emergency retract switch	Off
GW arming	Off
GW PAIRS/SINGLE switch	As required
Auxiliary warning panel	All lights on except TTC. Test for TTC lights. NIGHT/DAY switch as required

COCKPIT – RIGHT CENTRAL SIDE

Navigation lights switch	As required
Taxi lamps	OFF
Camera iris switch	As required
Camera master switch	As required
* De-ice switch	OFF (warning light out)
+ De-ice/rain dispersal switch	OFF (warning light out)
Pitot heater switch	On (forward)
Front and side windscreen heating switches	ON
Engine starter master switch	ON
Standby inverter switch	NORMAL
Ignition switches	ON
Cabin air switch	Off
Battery switch	ON
Cockpit lamps	As required
Nozzle position indicators	Check
IFF master switch	ON
IFF control panel	Standby
Autopilot master switch	ON
Auto stabilizers	OFF
ILS/ATT.HOLD	ATT.HOLD
Fuel switches	Both back (AWP fuel lights out) Both forward (lights remain out)
Cabin temp. selector	As required
Cabin altitude	Check altimeter

Brake accumulator pressure
   gauge | 2,000 psi (min)
Instrument master switch | ON (caged)

CONTROL COLUMN

Autopilot	OFF (central)
Armament trigger safety catch	SAFE
Brake lever	On, parking catch engaged

STARTING THE ENGINES

Confirm or set

Brakes	ON
Instrument master switch	ON (Inverter indicator white)
SWS mute button	Down
HP cocks/throttles	Idle/Fast idle
Battery switch	ON
Fuel switches	PORT – No. 1 engine STBD – No. 2 engine (Both forward)
Engine start master switch	ON
Nos 1 and 2 ignition switches	ON
No. 1 engine start button	Press for 2 seconds and release

CHECKS AFTER STARTING No. 1 ENGINE

JPT	700° C max
Fire warning	Out
Oil pressure warning	Out above 45% rpm
Hydraulic warning (No. 1 and SWP)	Out above 40% rpm
Flaps and airbrakes	Test

STARTING No. 2 ENGINE

| No. 2 engine starter button | Press for 2 seconds and release |

CHECKS AFTER STARTING No. 2 ENGINE

JPT	700° C max
Fire warning	Out
Oil pressure warning	Out above 45% rpm
Hydraulic warning (No. 2)	Out above 40% rpm
Ground supply	Disconnect
AC and TURB failure warning	Out at 58% rpm
SWP and AWP	Increase rpm if necessary on No. 1 engine and check all warnings out

Notes – With an engine at max rpm, 50% or above must be maintained on the other engine. Single engine running on No. 1 must be kept to a minimum. Maintain No. 2 engine at fast idling for AC electrical supply.

FAILURE TO START

NO INITIATION – repeat starting checks, wait one minute and try again. No limit to the number of attempts.

INITIATION BUT ENGINE DOES NOT TURN – wait one minute but no longer and then make a further attempt. Up to six attempts may be made as the heat factor is not present.

ENGINE ROTATES BUT FAILS TO LIGHT UP – HP cock/throttle – CLOSE. Wait one minute and make second attempt, if possible ensuring waste fuel has drained. If second attempt fails wait 45 minutes before making a further attempt.

Note – The HP cock must be closed immediately it is seen that the engine will not light up. The HP cock should be closed before the rpm reduce to 10%.

AFTER START CHECKS

Canopy	Check lights on. Select closed. Shoot bolts LOCKED. Lights out
Standby inverter indicator	Black
Flight instruments	Attitude indicator and standby art. horizon erected. Mk.5 FT compass set. Altimeter set
Autopilot magnetic indicator	Black
Brake pressure	3,000 psi

Cabin air switch	ON
Anti-G	Test
SWP	Test – cancel. All warning lights out
AWP	Test, release, all warning lights out
Ice warning light	Out

TAKE-OFF CHECKS

Trim	Rudder neutral, Aileron neutral, Tailplane – TO
Airbrakes	In and locked
Autopilot	Master SUPPLIES switch ON. Autostabilizers ON. ILS, ATT. HOLD – ATT. HOLD. Control column switch OFF. Throttle servo UNLOCK
Fuel	Contents
Flaps	Up and indicated
Instruments	Mk.5 compass synchronized. Attitude indicator and standby art. horizon erected. Other instruments normal. Inverter indicator black. Pitot heater ON. SWP and AWP warning lights out
Oxygen	Contents/100%. Pressure. Flow indicator – operation. Flow check
Hood	Closed. Shoot bolts LOCKED. Warning lights out
Harness	Tight and locked
Hydraulics	Warnings out. Check controls for full and free movement

TAKE-OFF

Parallel No. 1 throttle with No. 2 and then open both to 85% rpm. Check that the brakes hold on a dry surface. Increase both throttles to maximum cold thrust releasing the brakes simultaneously. Check nozzles move to closed position and JPT at least 650° C. If not, abandon take-off.

Notes

The brakes will not hold maximum cold thrust.

If icing conditions prevail use anti-icing during take-off. If runway length is insufficient (less than 6,000 ft) for the use of anti-icing, run the engines at 85% for one minute with anti-icing ON, then switch OFF before take-off.

Rudder 'q' feel will automatically cut in when the undercarriage is raised.

If an engine fails at or below Vstop, abandon the take-off. Vstop in ICAO conditions on a 2,500 yd runway, zero wind and no runway slope using full braking with brake parachute streamed is 140 knots on a wet runway and 160 knots on a dry runway. In temperate summer conditions (+27° C) on a 2,400 yd runway, zero wind and no slope using full braking with the brake parachute streamed, the Vstop on a wet runway is 129 knots and on a dry runway 150 knots.

Unstick speed is 165–170 knots.

CHECKS AFTER TAKE-OFF

Brakes	Apply momentarily
Undercarriage	UP (before 250 kts)
Ventral tank (if fitted)	Magnetic indicator black
AI: Transmitter	ON
Auto-range lever	Back
Phase change	SEARCH
Scale change	28 nm
ACM switch	Inboard

DESCENT AND APPROACH PROCEDURES

FAST DESCENT

Speed	1.1 M/450 knots
Airbrakes	Out
Power	Idle/Idle

NORMAL DESCENT

Speed	0.9 M/350 knots
Airbrakes	Out
Power	Idle/Fast Idle

RANGE DESCENT

Speed	0.9 M/250 knots
Airbrakes	In
Power	Idle/Idle (but if AC warning, No. 2 engine to fast idle)

SINGLE ENGINE DESCENT

As for two-engine descents, but live engine to be at fast idle.

INSTRUMENT APPROACH SETTINGS

TWO ENGINES WITH VENTRAL TANK AND MISSILES

Stage	% rpm (approx.)	Speed (kts)	Flaps	U/C	Airbrakes
Level	82–82	250–190	Down	Down	Out
Glideslope	80–80	190–175	Down	Down	Out

SINGLE ENGINE

Stage	% rpm (approx.)	Speed (kts)	Flaps	U/C	Airbrakes
Level	95	250–190	Down	Down	Out
Glideslope	93	190–175	Down	Down	Out

AIRCRAFT APPROACH LIMITATION

GCA   325 ft indicated above runway level. 300 feet true.

LANDING AND SHUT DOWN CHECKS

CHECKS BEFORE LANDING

Airbrakes	OUT
Undercarriage	DOWN, below 220 knots. Three green lights
Fuel	Contents, 400 lb/side min
Flaps	DOWN
Harness	Tight and locked
Brake pressure	3,000 psi min
Speeds	Approach 190–180 kts. Threshold 165 kts. Touchdown 155 kts

IMMEDIATELY AFTER TOUCHDOWN

Both throttles	Idle/Fast Idle
Nosewheel	Lower on to runway
Brake parachute handle	Pull to full extent

AFTER LANDING

Brake parachute	Jettison at 10 kts
No. 1 throttle/HP cock	HP cock closed when stopped

When No. 1 engine stopped

Flaps	UP
Airbrakes	IN
Electrical services	Switch off non-essential services

Taxi back with No. 2 engine at fast idle.

SHUT-DOWN CHECKS

Brakes	Parking brake on
No. 2 throttle/HP cock	HP cock closed
Fuel switches	OFF
All electrical services	Off
Ejection seat	Safe for parking
Battery switch	OFF
Cockpit lighting	Off

Lightning F.1 and F.1A Emergency Drills, July 1961

ENGINE AND REHEAT FIRES

ENGINE FIRE (F1 or F2 warning)

Close appropriate throttle/HP cock. Switch fuel to remaining engine. Reduce speed (IAS) if practicable. Press appropriate fire extinguisher. Land as soon as possible.

If warning disappears: Test the SWP system and if unserviceable proceed as for persistent fire.

If warning persists: If an F1 warning, jettison the ventral tank. Look for signs of fire. If signs of fire are apparent such as smoke, flame, control system malfunction or instrument indication: Abandon the aircraft.

Note – A visual check by another aircraft will be of assistance. If the other fire warning comes on no extinguishant will be available and the aircraft must be abandoned. Do not attempt to relight after fire warning.

SINGLE REHEAT WARNING (RHT1 OR RHT2)

Cancel reheat on both engines.

If the warning goes out: Test the SWP system and if unserviceable proceed as for persistent warning. Continue the flight using minimum power on both engines. Land as soon as possible.

If the warning persists: Close appropriate throttle/HP cock. Switch fuel to remaining engine.

If the warning still persists: Look for signs of fire. Use minimum power necessary for the remainder of the flight. If RHT1 warning, jettison the ventral tank. If signs of fire are apparent such as smoke or flame, control system malfunction or instrument indication: Abandon the aircraft.

DOUBLE REHEAT WARNING (RHT1 and RHT2)

Cancel reheat on both engines. Continue the flight using minimum power necessary. Land as soon as possible.

If one warning persists: Stop the appropriate engine. Switch fuel to remaining engine. If RHT1 persists, jettison the ventral tank.

If the warnings go out: Test the SWP system and if unserviceable proceed as for persistent warning.

If both warnings persist, abandon the aircraft.

ABANDONING

SEAT LIMITATIONS

Minimum speed	90 knots
Minimum altitude	Ground level in level or climbing flight
Recommended speed	250 knots

ACTIONS

Reduce speed to 250 knots if possible. Straight and level or climbing flight. Seat fully down. Pull primary or secondary firing handle.

Note: If above 42,000 ft and circumstances permit, depressurize for 3 seconds before ejecting

FAILURE OF AUTO-SEPARATION

Pull manual override D-ring to full extent. Pull up manual separation lever on port side of seat pan. Roll out of seat and when clear pull parachute D-ring. Emergency oxygen will not be available once separated from seat.

ENGINE FAILURE AND RELIGHTING

ENGINE FAILURE ON TAKE-OFF

The take-off should be abandoned if an engine failure occurs at or below
V$_{STOP}$.

Engine failure at or below V$_{STOP}$

Throttle	Back to idle/fast idle
Brake parachute	Stream
HP cocks	Closed
Wheel brakes	Apply maximum pressure
Runway safety barrier	Call to raise

Engine failure above V$_{STOP}$

Throttle	Both max. cold thrust
Undercarriage	Up as soon as possible when airborne
Failed engine	HP cock closed
Fuel switches	Selected to good engine

Engine failure during flight –mechanical defect

Throttle/HP cock	HP cock closed
Fuel switches	Selected to good engine

Do not relight

Engine failure during flight –flame out

Relight button	Press for 2 seconds

If rpm do not rise within 20 seconds:

Throttle/HP cock	HP cock closed

Carry out relighting drill

RELIGHTING

Speed	0.9 M max
Altitude	30,000 ft max or 40,000 ft max post Avon Mod.2262
Throttle	HP cock closed
Fuel switches	To appropriate engines
Engine master switch	ON
Ignition switch	ON
Relight button	Press for 2 seconds
Throttle	Idling

If no relight occurs after 20 seconds, close the HP cock and repeat the drill at a lower altitude and speed.

JETTISON PROCEDURES

VENTRAL TANK JETTISONING

Position over safe area if possible. If below 25,000 ft reduce speed to 0.8 M. Ideal speed is 250 knots. Pull ventral tank jettison handle.

Note : If 0.8 M is exceeded during jettisoning below 25,000 ft violent nose-down pitching could exceed negative g structural limits.

MISSILE JETTISONING

Reduce to below the limits 300 knots subsonic/2 g if possible. Position over safe area if possible. Lift safety catch on ventral tank jettison and squeeze exposed lever. Do not pull ventral tank jettison handle unless the tank also has to be jettisoned.

CANOPY JETTISONING

Reduce speed to 300 knots or below. Lower the seat. Keep head down. Pull canopy jettison handle to full extent. If canopy fails to jettison after pulling the normal canopy jettison handle, or on ejection after pulling the primary or secondary firing handles, operate the emergency canopy jack release lever and then pull up the normal canopy opening handle.

PRESSURIZATION AND HEATING FAILURES

PRESSURIZATION FAILURE

Descend immediately to 25,000 ft or below. Switch off AI. If fuel permits return to base at 20,000 ft or below and 350 knots. Use ram air as necessary for ventilation.

OVERHEATING

Select MANUAL on temperature controller and hold at COOL for 10–15 seconds. If successful, leave at MANUAL. If overheating persists, proceed as for pressurization failure and select CABIN AIR-OFF.

OVERCOOLING

Select MANUAL on temperature controller and hold at WARM for 10–15 seconds. If successful, leave at MANUAL. If overcooling persists, proceed as for pressurization failure and select CABIN AIR-OFF.

SMOKE IN COCKPIT

If smoke is coming from the air diffusers select CABIN AIR-OFF. If smoke is coming from another source select ram air valve open. In both cases proceed as for pressurization failure. Select emergency at the oxygen regulator and oxygen mask toggle down.

MIST IN COCKPIT

Select DEMIST to ALL ON.

POWER CONTROLS FAILURE

No. 1 Controls system (HYD1) – Reduce speed if practicable. Do not exceed 2 g. Return and land immediately. Carry out normal approach and landing. Select brake parachute and apply maximum braking.

Note – Emergency undercarriage system will be inoperative. If the failure is due to flame-out of the No. 1 engine, windmilling rpm may provide accumulator pressure for streaming the brake parachute.

No. 2 Controls system (HYD2) – Reduce speed if practicable. Do not exceed 2 g. Return to base and carry out a normal approach and landing.

Both controls system (HYD1 and HYD2) – Prepare to abandon the aircraft.

Note – If the failure is due to a double engine flame-out, windmilling rpm at 250 knots or above may provide sufficient hydraulic pressure for limited control before abandoning.

SERVICES SYSTEM FAILURE

The following Services will be inoperative – 1) Undercarriage normal system, 2) Flaps, 3) Airbrakes, 4) GE and RP, 5) Canopy operation, 6) Nose-wheel centring and anti-shimmy, 7) Feel simulator, 8) Autostabilizers and autopilot, 9) Brakes.

Note 5–9 – Accumulator pressure may be available. (Brakes, check brake pressure gauge)

Actions – Airbrakes – IN, Return to base and set up approach for flap-less landing. Use emergency system to lower undercarriage. Increase threshold speed by 10 knots. Stream brake parachute and close HP cocks immediately on touchdown. Apply continuous pressure without maxaretting in one application of the wheel brakes. Do not taxi.

Note – The landing should be made at an airfield with a long runway (minimum 7,500 ft) equipped with a safety barrier.

FUEL PRESSURE WARNING

Below 10,000 ft
Cancel reheat, restrict engine rpm and reduce speed until warning is cancelled. If warning remains on – do not accelerate engine above 85% rpm. Reduce speed to a practicable minimum. Do not run the affected engine above 10,000 ft.

Above 10,000 ft
Range Critical – Continue normal recovery on two engines. If engine flames out: close HP cock of the affected engine. Attempt a relight when below 10,000 ft. If relight unsuccessful, switch fuel to the good engine. If fuel warning appears on the good engine side restrict engine rpm and speed to a practicable minimum and remain below 10,000 ft.

Range not critical – Close the HP cock of the affected engine. Continue recovery on one engine. Do not switch fuel to remaining engine nor attempt a relight above 10,000 ft.

FUEL ASYMMETRY DURING SINGLE-ENGINE FLYING

To check the serviceability of the non-feeding side carry out the following drill: Fly below 30,000 ft and 0.9 M. Check ignition switches and engine start master switch – ON. Check that fuel switches are both selected to the live engine. Press the relight button of the live engine for 2 seconds and release. Switch off the fuel switch on the feeding side. Wait for 5 seconds with the switch at OFF or until the fuel pressure warning light appears, then return the switch to its former position.

Note – If a fuel warning does not appear all fuel will be available to the live engine. If a fuel warning appears, fuel on the non-feeding side may be available to the live engine, depending on the type of failure. Before attempting to feed the fuel, reduce height to 10,000 ft or below and switch off the feeding side just before it empties.

VENTRAL TANK TRANSFER WARNING

Gentle manoeuvres only and turns up to 60 degrees bank and 2 g are permitted. Rolling manoeuvres are not permitted. Additionally, if missiles are carried, reduce speed to 250 knots on descending below 35,000 ft. Land as soon as possible.

UNDERCARRIAGE EMERGENCIES

Check serviceability of services hydraulic system by selecting airbrakes OUT and then IN.

Undercarriage fails to unlock (ALL U/C lights out) – Reselect several times. If unsuccessful, use emergency down whether services system is serviceable or not. If the undercarriage still fails to unlock it is recommended that the aircraft is abandoned.

Undercarriage unlocks but fails to lock down (one or more U/C red lights) – If services system is unserviceable, use emergency down. If services system is serviceable: Try reselection. Ascertain position of U/C legs from control tower or another aircraft. If a U/C leg is within 20 degrees of fully down, yaw the aircraft for periods of at least 20 seconds favourable to that leg (i.e. yaw to starboard to lock port leg), increasing speed into the range 270–280 knots. The maximum benefit of yaw is obtained in this speed band. If leg was stopped at a higher position, use roll first and then yaw. If still unsuccessful, select emergency down.

Use of emergency selection – Maintain level or climbing flight with minimum use of control column. Speed 180 knots. Run No. 1 engine at highest practicable power commensurate with speed and configuration, and at least at 70% rpm, until the undercarriage is locked down. If still unsuccessful, proceed as in above paragraph.

Landing with a main wheel or wheels unlocked – A landing should not be attempted. Abandon the aircraft.

Landing with both main wheels locked down but nosewheel unlocked – Jettison the ventral tank and all jettisonable stores and on the final approach to land at a speed above 200 knots and with flaps up, the canopy. Select flaps if available. When the main wheels touch, stream the brake parachute, holding a nose-high attitude for maximum aerodynamic braking. Shut the HP cocks. Lower the nose on to the runway before tailplane control is lost. Apply the brakes to keep straight. If a barrier is in use on the runway, have it in the down position.

ELECTRICAL FAILURES

ALTERNATOR FAILURE

Immediate – Cancel reheat (if not cancelled automatically). Throttle back smoothly. Descend to 27,000 ft using the standby altimeter.

Subsequent –

Pitot heater	STANDBY
Inverter	STANDBY
Autopilot	Master switch OFF

Continue descent to 22,000 ft or lower if fuel permits and to 10,000 ft or lower if fuel is at or below 500 lb/side. Use the standby altimeter throughout.

Services Inoperative – Windscreen heaters and canopy blower, AI, armament circuits, TACAN, main altimeter, fuel vent valve heaters, AC fuel booster pumps, TTC, IFF, Autopilot.

GENERATOR FAILURE

Immediate – Cancel reheat. Throttle back smoothly. If no voltmeter fitted: descend at max rate to 10,000 ft or VMC below cloud, whichever is the lower. Shed non-essential DC loads. If voltmeter is fitted and is reading more than 23 volts: Shed non-essential DC loads and monitor voltmeter. Descend and then cruise at 0.9 M/36,000 ft. When voltmeter falls to 23 volts descend at max rate to 10,000 ft or VMC below cloud, whichever is lower.

Subsequent – Maintain 85% rpm or lower on both engines. If fuel permits, select undercarriage down and check green lights before battery is exhausted.

BATTERY FAILURE

Maintain 85% rpm or lower on both engines. Only available flight instruments are E.2 compass, standby altimeter, ASI, Machmeter and rate of climb indicator. Fuel gauges will underread with declining voltage and then fall to zero. Use emergency system to lower the undercarriage. The brake parachute can be streamed but will not be jettisonable. Flaps will be inoperative. Trimmers will be inoperative. If an engine flames out it may not be possible to relight it. The fuel switches will be inoperative. SWP and AWP will be inoperative.

AIR TURBINE OR GENERATOR AND ALTERNATOR FAILURE

Immediate – Cancel reheat (if not cancelled automatically). Throttle back smoothly. If no voltmeter fitted: descend at max rate to 10,000 ft or VMC below cloud, whichever is lower, using the standby altimeter. Shed non-essential DC loads. If voltmeter fitted and is reading more than 23 volts: descend at max rate to 27,000 ft. Shed non-essential DC loads and monitor the voltmeter. When voltmeter falls to 23 volts continue the descent at max rate to 10,000 ft or VMC below cloud, whichever is lower, using the standby altimeter.

Subsequent – Maintain 85% rpm or lower on both engines.

Pitot heater	STANDBY
Standby artificial horizon	STANDBY
Inverter	STANDBY

If fuel permits select undercarriage down and check green lights before battery is exhausted.

NON-ESSENTIAL DC LOADS

ILS	11 amp
Non-essential VHF/UHF	6/11 amp
AI	3 amp
Navigation lights	2.7 amp
Autopilot	2.7 amp
IFF	2 amp
Master armament selector	2 amp
Camera heater	2 amp
Cockpit lighting	1.2 amp
Tacan	1 amp

Lightning Conversion Squadron – Syllabus, September 1962

Convex No. 1 (Dual) Duration 40 min
1) Full cold power take-off
2) Climb to FL 360
3) Accelerate to 1.3 M
4) Handling at 1.3 M
5) Handling at 0.95 M
6) At 1,600/1,600 lb recover under GCI to the Dive Circle
7) Carry out GCI/GCA monitoring on TACAN
8) Overshoot into second GCA, and land

Convex No. 2 (Dual) Duration 45 min
1) Cold power climb to FL 360
2) Handle at 0.95 M with and without autostabs and feel
3) Recover at 1,800/1,800 lb using TACAN/GCA
4) Overshoot from GCA into visual circuits
5) Carry out visual circuits and overshoots until landing at 800/800 lb

Convex No. 3 (Dual) Duration 30 min
1) Reheat take-off. Cancel reheat at 10,000 ft
2) Climb to FL360
3) Accelerate to 1.6 M
4) Handling at 1.6 M with variable reheat

5) Decelerate and cruise to Dive Circle
6) TACAN/ILS recovery
7) Land off ILS

Convex No. 4 (Dual) Duration 45 min
1) Cold power climb to FL 360
2) Maximum rate turns with and without reheat within the 'g' and buffet limits
3) Descend to FL 100 and throttle one engine to slow idle
4) Single-engined handling and TACAN recovery
5) Single-engined ILS or GCA followed by a single-engined over-shoot
6) Normal and flapless circuits and overshoots
7) Single-engined landing at 800/800 lb

Convex No. 5 (Solo) Duration 40 min
1) Full cold power take-off
2) Climb to FL 360
3) Handling at 1.3 M
4) Handling at 0.95 M
5) Recover at 1,600/1,600 lb with GCI to the Dive Circle
6) Two GCA approaches, landing from the second

Convex No. 6 (Solo) Duration 45 min – as Convex No. 2

Convex No. 7 (Solo) Duration 30 min – as Convex No. 3

Convex No. 8 (Solo) Duration 35 min
1) Cold climb at 450 kts/0.9 M to the service ceiling, i.e. until the rate of climb falls to less than 1,000 ft per minute
2) When service ceiling is reached, note height
3) Maintaining 0.9 M, engage max reheat and note the new service ceiling
4) Descend to FL 360 accelerating to 1.5 M and using max reheat, zoom at 15 degrees to 50,000 ft
5) Handling at 50,000 ft
6) Carry out a GCI/Dive Circle/ILS recovery monitoring on TACAN
7) If over 1,000/1,000 lb, overshoot into a visual circuit

Convex No. 9 (Solo) Duration 1 hour
1) TACAN XC to the Dive Circle
2) ILS or GCA landing

Convex No. 10 (Dual) Duration 35 min
1) Climb to FL 360
2) Accelerate to 1.6 M
3) 15 degree climb to FL 560
4) Handle at FL 560
5) Descend to FL 360 at 1.1 M with airbrakes out, idle/ fast idle set
6) Descend to FL 100 carrying out aerobatics as briefed
7) Recover on TACAN to a visual circuit

Convex No. 11 (Solo) Duration 45 min
1) Climb to FL 360
2) Simulate total radio failure
3) Recover to base on TACAN/ILS
4) Practice diversion to crash diversion on the standby UHF set
5) Return to base on TACAN

Convex No. 12 (Dual) Duration 50 min
AI familiarization sortie using a Canberra from the Target Facility Squadron as target

SUMMARY
Sorties prior to solo – 4. Hours prior to solo – 2.40. Total hours solo – 4.15.
Total hours dual – 4.05. Total hours – 8.20 in 12 sorties

Index

XN734 62
XN772 86
XN774 88
XN775 99
XN776 99
XN777 99
XN783 89
XN789 133
XN793 99
XN794 132

XP693 62, 76, 133
XP694 62
XP695 68
XP696 68
XP697 71, 81
XP699 62
XP700 100
XP 705 94

XP739 103
XP741 100
XP749 68
XP750 68
XP760 89

XR711 101
XR714 101
XR763 103
XR766 85
XR769 96
XR771 98
XR773 91

XS896 92–3
XS938 93

55–710 102